Drake University Marching Band, Don R. Marcouiller, Director

marching for marching bands

marching

FOR MARCHING BANDS

don r. marcouiller

Director of Bands
Drake University

WM. C. BROWN COMPANY • Publishers • Dubuque, Iowa

87398

Manufactured by WM. C. BROWN CO. INC., Dubuque, Iowa
Printed in U. S. A.

acknowledgements

The author respectfully dedicates this book to many teachers and friends who have had a real part in its formulation. A partial list of some of these names might read as follows: Robert Petzold, Samuel T. Burns, Emmett Sarig, Stan Stitgen, C. H. Beebe, Lester Skornicka, Roger Muzzy, Roger Miller, and Al Gillespie.

Special mention must be given to Ray Dvorak, Director of Bands, University of Wisconsin, for his invaluable help as a teacher and friend, and to "Edgewood," a term which encompasses the spirit of a devoted faculty and wonderful student body with which the author was privileged to have been associated.

contents

chapter   I—Introduction   page 1

chapter   II—The Components—Marching and Music   6

chapter   III—Showmanship   12

chapter   IV—Applied Showmanship   16

chapter   V—Form   25

chapter   VI—The Habitat   29

chapter   VII—The Small Unit Turn   32

chapter   VIII—The Double Series Turn   41

chapter   IX—Entrance Maneuvers   50

chapter   X—Progressive File Maneuvers   70

chapter   XI—Minstrel Turn Maneuvers   74

chapter   XII—File Maneuvers   **78**

chapter   XIII—The Formation of Pinwheels   82

chapter   XIV—Pinwheel Maneuvers   87

chapter   XV—Stationary Formation Charts   95

chapter   XVI—Charting Formation Breaks   101

chapter   XVII—Basic Drill   106

Appendix—Outstanding College Bands   117

Bibliography   129

chapter 1

Introduction

America means many things to many people. Freedom, opportunity, democracy . . . . . or perhaps more simply, home, friends, church, the local ball club, or crys of, "On Wisconsin!" and "Go You Packers!" Changing seasons bring changing meanings. Fads come and go, but some reoccurring pastimes intrench themselves in the hearts of the nation, henceforth to be known as traditions.

The marching band is a part of one of these great traditions. Each fall the pulse of the nation rises and falls with the fortunes of its favorite football team. Alumni return to alma mater to relive for a few moments the spell of college or high school days; the team, the cheerleaders, the enthusiastic roar of the crowd, and the band. . . . The football stadium with all its color is truly an American tradition, a tradition inspired by the most powerful force of any nation, her people.

The marching band is very much a part of American football. Books might be written on the origins of the marching band on the football field, but it is not expedient to trace this history here. Suffice to say that at the precise moment in history when football was becoming a part of the school program, bands were in existence and were capable of playing for football fans. The ready-made audience has always had performance appeal. It was only a matter of time until the entertainment resources of the band found its way to the halftime gridiron. Since the first venture in the 1920's the band has become an increasing part of the "pageant" of football.

The union of football and band has been a logical one, of profit to both partners. To football is added color and keen school spirit aroused and kept alive by the school band. The advent of the band's halftime performance brought a new and greater entertainment value to the spectacle.

Perhaps greater change has been wrought in the band movement by its association with the football stadium. The term "marching band," once evoked the impression of a military band accompanying marching troops, or perhaps, a military review. Today the term is more likely to be inseparable from the impression of the gridiron. Suffice to say that the marching band has been profoundly influenced by football.

Much has been said about the educational value of the present day football-marching band, or in cases, the lack thereof. To the value side of the ledger its protagonists point out the public relations value of marching performances both in popularizing the music program and the school itself. While few hold the type of music performed to be of significant value, many contend that the performance itself is of great motivational value to the bandsman and to the young potential bandsman who is frequently introduced to a fine music program through the medium of the marching band. Practical experiences in cooperation, the discipline of fitting into a group, belonging, and pride of membership in a fine organization are undoubtedly values to be weighed against the "debit" side of the marching band ledger.

Its critics point out the fact that the marching band, as we have come to know it, bears little relation to music education. While bands attempt to play well as they march, their repertoire is necessarily limited, and consequently may not possess great value as good music. It is often felt that the time spent on marching activities is out of proportion with the value to be derived from the activity, with the consequent feeling that this time might better be spent in the music classrooms.

In brief, the controversy might be summarized as time spent vs. value received. As is the case with most controversies, the individual solution is often colored by local conditions. Where conditions have been conducive to large stadia and football crowds the marching band has usually thrived.

No attempt is made here to present a defense of the marching band. Like football itself, much will be said pro and con in days to come, but one thing seems certain; it is here to stay! It may undergo a certain degree of revision or reemphasis, but it is a safe prediction to say that any activity as popular as football and the marching band will not be easily abolished from the rank of tradition until the people themselves lose interest. Football, like baseball, is a national tradition of long standing. As long as football persists it also seems

University of Michigan Band, William D. Revelli, Director

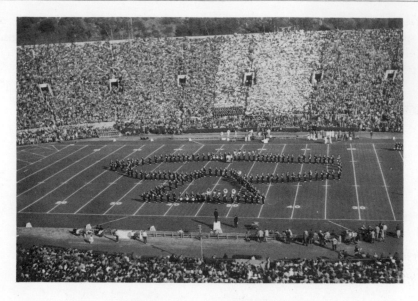

University of Wisconsin Band

reasonable to predict that no major change will be made in the status of the marching band.

Directors of bands must be prepared to meet the challenge of the gridiron. More people will see their work here than on the concert stage. More people will judge the music program of the school on the basis of the marching band than on the concert organizations. The marching band is, in a sense then, the showcase of the music program. Its function may be closely akin to entertainment, but it is not entertainment in the cheap definition of the word. It is of a wholesome type often hinged upon school spirit, loyalty, patriotism, or appeals in the public interest. The marching band is real. It is a part of the music program. For better or for worse its leaders must be prepared to meet its challenge.

It is sincerely hoped that the following chapters will be useful to the marching band director in moulding his music-marching program. The nature of the job to be performed and the tools with which he must work will be discussed at some length. The halftime performance will be viewed from the standpoint of the director, the spectator and the bandsman. The place of motion and marching will be discussed as it relates to the halftime performance. Finally the closing chapters will be devoted to a presentation of a new concept of precision marching developed by the author and presented originally by the University of Wisconsin Marching Band and more recently by the Drake University Marching Band.

The Components — Marching and Music

The obvious components of the marching band are marching and music. Without marching we have a concert band; without music we have a drill team. These statements seem the epitomy of simplicity, yet when the inter-relation of the components is discussed, simplicity gives way to complexity. Which, for instance, is more important; the marching, or the music?

If the question is directed to the layman in the football stadium on a brisk fall afternoon the answer is usually a resounding vote for marching. When it is directed to the music educator the answer is likely to be emphatically music. Ask the director of the marching band and you are speaking to a fellow who must tread the narrow path between the opinions of the audience, the educator, and his own convictions.

Chapter II seeks a more clearly defined answer to the question through a discussion of the problem as seen by the layman, the educator, and the director.

To the layman the main interest of the marching band is *visual*. He might go to the concert hall and close his eyes to listen to the music, but he does not close them in the stadium. It is more likely that he figuratively closes his ears, for it is true that he frequently may not be able to recall what music was played at halftime, but only seldom is he unable to recall what he saw. Musicians too. often become absorbed in the visual area of a halftime performance with the result that the mind focuses on what is seen to the exclusion of other areas of the performance. A movie is an expression of this same situation. Few people attending a movie which features fine music can intelligently recall its presence later.

The layman can easily grasp the objective of a group marching, for he is immediately conscious of a pattern and of feet moving to-

Black Knights Drum and Bugle Corps, Belleville, Illinois Forrest T. Creson, Director

gether. Alignment and precision of movement is also obvious to him. Imperfection in the set pattern is, unfortunately, equally obvious; as a matter of fact, he is likely to seek out imperfection immediately. Because the objective of perfection is apparent to the viewer, he is more than likely to judge the performance by the number of errors he detects than by a more objective standard. The ability of the layman to grasp this standard defines the criteria by which marching is judged; a standard of perfection, or an absolute one.

Music on the other hand, is more intangible. It must be judged by a standard relative to the musical experience and the maturity of the listener. The individual may have his conception of perfection, but there is no reason to believe this conception will correspond with that of another. An absolute standard of musical perfection is an abstraction incapable of human definition.

The layman watching a halftime performance can easily detect very poor music or very excellent music, but the middle shades of mediocrity are often beyond his capacity to distinguish. It does not seem presumptuous to say then, that the spectator, who in the last analysis is the judge of the performance, evaluates music on a less severe standard than on the absolute one with which he judges marching. It seems that, to an audience, "marching is the thing."

Applying this knowledge to concrete situations, however, often gives rise to new problems. Take the case of a hypothetical band that has just performed quite well on the football field, having ten errors in marching and ten errors in music as noted by two visiting band directors. When the director is informed of the ten errors in each area he has a decision to make. There is not enough time available before the next performance to "iron out" both music and marching errors. On which should he concentrate?

Being familiar with the comparison standards of an audience, this director concentrated on marching errors, knowing they were more obvious to the audience. Since the musical errors were noted by musicians it seemed possible that the audience was less conscious of them anyway. Perhaps this director's friends criticised him for playing no better at the next performance, but it seems certain that the audience went away happy over the band's fine performance. The position that the director now finds himself in illustrates the basic controversy over the importance of music and marching. It is also at this point that the educator enters the discussion.

A Novel Street Formation, Black Knights Corps, Belleville, Illinois

The music educator considers marching as a fortunate or unfortunate part of the music program.   Music is the element that justifies the marching band activity.   It is most likely that music will also be the standard by which he judges the marching band performance. His emphasis on music then, bears all the weight of educational aims and objectives.   Criticism of this sort, however, carried beyond the limits defined by the marching band activity is diametrically opposed

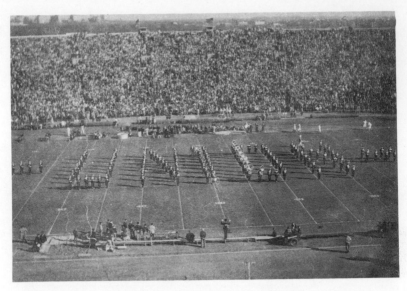

University of Wisconsin Band

to the evaluation characteristics of an audience. If music is to be the basic area for the evaluation of the educational values of the marching band, successful performances must represent a compromise between educational objectives and audience appeal.

A narrow music standard of judgment loses sight of the basic activity of the marching band. *Music must lose some of its lustre the moment marching enters in.* Marching is a qualifying feature which compromises the highest standards of music, as indeed, does carrying a bulky instrument limit the highest standards of marching. The marching band is compounded of two basically incompatible activities, music and marching. Each must lose some of its original identity in combining to form the new and completely different element. The new element must be evaluated educationally on its own merits. It seems as silly to evaluate the music of the marching band on preconceived standards of the concert band as it does to evaluate water by the taste of hydrogen and oxygen. Music assumes a functional or secondary importance in the marching band. It is truly, *music for marching.* Its relation to marching might be typified by the state-ment, "Where the marching band is concerned, people listen with their eyes."

It is only fitting that this discussion close with the admonition that it is impossible to have a fine organization with a noticeable lack in either area.   The relative standard of music should be no quarter for mediocrity.   It does serve, however, as a valuable guide in the preparation of a halftime performance.   A fine marching band with poor music is as pathetic a creation as the fine musical group that marches poorly.

Music for the marching band should be chosen, arranged, and *evaluated* with the needs of the marching band in mind.   It should fit into the general scope and pattern of the activity, and finally, *it should be played in the very best possible manner* under the existing conditions.

chapter III

Showmanship

Marching and music have been defined in the previous chapter. It seems logical that attention now be shifted to showmanship which is closely associated with both areas. Webster defines showmanship as, "the quality of showing or exhibiting something to advantage." Such is its function here.

The term "showmanship" seems to have fallen into a state of disrepute. It may tend to be synonymous with an expression of cheapness in many minds. Certainly the term deserves a better reputation. Actually it has been a part of music since the world's first performer picked up his reed or shell. It is a part of every performance of the most humble or of the finest music. Opera and ballet could not function without it. The use of the term should cause no raised eyebrows when applied to the marching band.

Once again it is easy to agree to the *principle* of showmanship, but the *application* is another story. Perhaps the term might be likened to spice added to food as a seasoning. Planned and added judiciously in proper amounts it is wonderful, but the moment it tends to replace the basic foods it becomes very unpalatable. How much spice to use? Any restaurateur can tell you no two chefs agree.

Showmanship is a matter of individual taste. The following list of groups have been added to some bands as a matter of individual taste.

1. twirlers	7. dancers	13. special instruments
2. flag swingers	8. rope swingers	14. drumstick ribbons
3. bon-bon girls	9. cape swingers	15. costumes
4. rifle squads	10. guidons	16. pyro-technics
5. rifle twirlers	11. flag groups	17. black light
6. color guards	12. sousaphone covers	18. spot lights

A Turn Well Suited to a Large Band. --State University of Iowa Band, Fred Ebbs, Director

Showmanship, by nature, does not include or exclude these tastes. The individual must choose for himself. Common sense serves as the guide. Baton twirling, for instance, was heralded as a great innovation in its infancy, but when baton twirlers began to out-number the band they were viewed in a less enthusiastic light. Sim-iliar experiences might be noted in other above areas. These are very tangible expressions of showmanship, however. It might as-sume the form of a very intangible nuance in the music or an almost imperceptible motion. Like many other vague terms showmanship is perhaps more understandable in its abuse than in its use. If used properly it often goes completely unnoticed. A showman with a mediocre voice will often convince an audience that he is the world's finest tenor, while a beautiful voice goes unnoticed because of a lack of it.

Like flattery, showmanship loses its lustre only when its presence is noted. It must be sincere and genuine. It must remain in the background. It must seek nothing for itself, but only to promote the general welfare of the activity it serves.

Showmanship is no better or worse than the activity it promotes. A train robber might go about his work with a flourish termed show-manship in every sense of the word. The novel or the awesome place little demand on the wares of the showman, but the routine and the commonplace tax these wares to the limit. Showmanship must be a planned part of every halftime performance. It should not be accidental. A mediocre routine may become an excellent one by recognizing its emotional appeal and by emphasizing it. Emo-tional appeals are the tools of the showman. Any or all of the following appeals might be solicited in the course of a season.

1. surprise	7. suspense
2. humor	8. gaiety
3. loyalty	9. pathos
4. patriotism	10. fear
5. religious	11. mystery
6. aesthetic	

Because showmanship constantly asks if there is a better way of presenting material it has brought about many changes in the march-ing band field. As better ways of executing basic movements have been created the basic Army Manual of marching has been discarded.

University of Wisconsin Band

It is responsible for the variety of music now published for the marching band and for the versatility of its activity.

Finally, showmanship demands constant evaluation and revision. When the novel becomes commonplace interest wanes. Variety is the byword of showmanship as it is the spice of life. A marching band like a heavy truck has a tendency to form a rut and to bog down. Showmanship must be the element that avoids these ruts from forming for in all reality a rut is nothing less than a grave with open ends.

chapter IV

Applied Showmanship

Emotional appeal, novelty, and variety have been discussed as the tools of showmanship. These elements will now be discussed as they apply to specific areas of the halftime performance.

Showmanship in Music

Music .is potentially the bands greatest source of emotional appeal. A few bars of a hymn might establish a mood quite different from "The Sugar Blues." It has the power to shift moods very readily. Setting, or adding a functional purpose to the action might be thought of as music's primary role. It may accomplish its goal through familiar or unfamiliar music. The former is generally more meaningful and, as such, is preferred. Popular songs add additional appeal and novelty to the action. Songs with varied meters are certainly to be preferred. The marching band is perfectly capable of marching in a triple as well as a duple meter. If music has a beat, or is a multiple of a beat that corresponds to the range of marching cadence, it may serve as music for marching. The "Lady of Spain," in three-four time; "Halls of Ivy," played in four-four or eight-eight time; or the latest popular "hit" played in a swing rhythm is standard repetoire for the modern marching band. What then is to become of the military march?

The military march is in no danger of being discarded as an archaic musical form. Few "thrills" in marching equal the sight of a band passing smartly by to the sound of a Sousa march. It is true, however, that most marches tend to sound alike to the layman. There is a definite limit to the interest which might be sustained through the continued use of military marches. It might be well to think of the march as a wonderful effect, but one that is also subject to the limitations of sustained interest.

Purdue University Marching Band, Al G. Wright, Director

Type or variety of repetoire is only one phase of showmanship as it might be applied to music. Interpretation is another area of the utmost importance. Dynamic contrast is very effective on the football field. As a general rule dynamics need to be over stressed to give the sound traveling a great distance from the listener proper articulation. Pianissimo playing often has the power to hold an audience spellbound. In general the dynamics is an area of the marching band performance that deserves more attention than it has traditionally received.

The arrangement of a number to be performed is of very great importance. Normally sixteen bars of a chorus are enough to establish a particular formation or idea. To play an entire chorus is often disastrous from a standpoint of monotony. Take for example, a band using a tune to establish a "punch line" of some sequence. As the music is recognized the audience laughs for perhaps five seconds. It is more than likely that the longer the music continues the less humorous the incident seems. In such cases it is well to establish the joke with a fragment of the song and to finish shortly after the crowd has digested the meaning. A fast moving continuity is normally to be desired.

There is hardly a chorus of a march or a popular song which cannot be shortened if desirable, by using only its opening and closing phrases. With a small amount of effort a tune can be lengthened or shortened by any fraction. Special endings added to a familiar strain serves to lengthen it and to add additional interest to it. Many times closing sections or phrases can be broadened out by doubling the beats per measure. This technique very frequently adds a great deal of interest. Some numbers lend themselves to various tempo and meter changes. Many such choruses have been played with eight bars in an augmented style of four or eight beats per bar instead of two, eight bars subdued at the regular tempo in stop time, and the final bars at full volume and standard tempo with the trumpets moving up an octave on the final notes. Here is a case of maximum interest and variety being added to a number without the services of a special arrangement.

Finally it is not necessary to have the full marching band play all the time. Small combos or ensembles present a wealth of variety and interest. Featured sections or soloists add as much to the football situation as they do to the concert stage.

Four Lakes Drum and Bugle Corps, Madison, Wisconsin
Paul Haack, Director   C. H. Beebe, Exec. Director

Showmanship in Marching

Marching appeals readily to many of the emotions or appeals listed previously. Like music, however, it is valuable to vary the appeal and the type of marching sequence for the perils of monotony spares nothing.

Long, involved countermarches and turns executed by large bands often qualify as monotonous for the basic motion is slow and dependent on halfstepping. Shorter, more varied sequences tend to be more effective. Many bands have succumbed to the temptation of dragging out a good idea. A frequent offender is the dance step. Many times when it is executed to a flavorful dance rhythm it is immediately effective, but when the same basic movement is repeated throughout an entire selection the hot-dog barker eventually steals the center of attention. Halfstepping and marking time is generally to be avoided for they slow down the movement of the continuity. Both may be excellent, however, if other action assumes the center of attention. In a stationary position marking time may help to create rather than reduce interest, but in a marching sequence, again typified by the countermarch, it seems better to eliminate the movement than to undergo the halfstepping. In the last analysis the interest of the audience must be the guide. If interest is maintained by a selection or a maneuver it matters little how much time the sequence consumes.

Marching may be varied through the use of varied fronts and contours. With modern techniques of utilizing yard lines for alignment, company fronts are as easy to march as the block formation. This will be discussed in detail later.

Tempo changes with corresponding pace adjustments add needed variety to many performances. In music, augmentation of beats per bar was suggested for variety. In marching, the same technique is most effective. It is possible to double the ordinary number of steps per bar or to take only one half of the normal steps. An example of this technique was illustrated by a sequence executed by the University of Wisconsin Band in the 1955 football season. The music established by one half of the band marching in two steps per bar was the first theme of "Simple Melody" made famous by Bing and Gary Crosby. The second theme, or the contrasting jazz tune was next played in the same cadence by the second group marching rapidly in four beats per bar. The final portion of the tune featured both groups playing together, but marching at contrasting tempi.

The final chapters are devoted to marching drills and maneuvers which are based on ideas that radiate showmanship. In a sense, this discussion of showmanship in marching will be resumed then.

Showmanship in Formations

Up to this point in the chapter, showmanship has been discussed as it relates to marching and music as separate entities. In reality, music and marching are seldom separated on the football field, for one is usually accompanied by the other. The "formation" or design so common to the modern marching band is sometimes the exception. When carried to an extreme, a performance based on a series of formations isolates marching to the function of changing formations and music to the formations alone. This system does not even approach full potential of the marching band, but it will remain for a later chapter to discuss it in more detail. Suffice to say now, that formations themselves tend to become monotonous if they depend on music alone to *sustain* interest. The keenest interest in a formation comes the moment before it becomes recognizable or in the first few seconds of its legibility. From this moment on interest wanes rapidly. Music helps sustain it, but unfortunately, its potential is limited. If music does not supply the necessary interest in a given formation, marching or movement must.

The director of a halftime performance can do no better than to analyze each moment of the performance, carefully evaluating the center of interest or attention. Thirty seconds of dullness can seem like eternity on the football field.

Sustained interest can easily be added to formations through several techniques. The most familiar of these is the "floating" formation. This technique involves nothing more than marching a formation as a unit. A difficulty presented by the new final position of the formation can be offset by forming another design in this position and moving it back to the original location. One formation can, of course, be floated back to its original position as a part of one sequence.

Marking time is another means of momentarily adding increased interest to a formation. Short sequences of contrasting steps are also effective. Simple facing movements often add new color effects to a formation. The changing features of the uniforms and instruments are often startling. This effect might be enhanced by turning letters or segments of the formation on alternate counts.

The so-called "animated" formation, or a formation with moving parts needs no recommendation here. The old faithful train formation with moving wheels and puffing smoke is a typical example of animation.

Lights attached to uniforms for night games, spot lights to accent movement, and the use of black light is a popular and simple way to "show off" a formation. Again, these methods need no further definition or recommendation here.

All formations do not need a "gimmic," but if interest needs a boost, it is encouraging to realize that it might be added in one of these ways with a minimum amount of effort.

Formation Breaks

A "formation break" is a term used to designate the method used to march into and out of a formation. Perhaps no section of the halftime performance is as neglected as this area. Chapter XVI deals with marching technics to add interest and variety to the "break," but it is well to discuss here the variety that might be added to it through the use of the public address system and through music.

The formation break is by nature the modulating passage of the marching band performance. It comes between two formations and is often considered unimportant. This seems an unfortunate view, for as in its musical counterpart, the modulating passage is often one of the most interesting parts of a composition.

If a public address system is used, it is frequently utilized at this point. This moment is certainly preferable to the use of the P.A. once a formation is formed and the band is standing idle. The latter situation takes the spontaneity out of continuity and tends to slow down its pace. If a very important announcement is used at this point for the sake of clarity, it is well to keep it as short as possible. Cleverly written, the P.A. script can do much to keep interest alive. There are many ways that it might be coordinated with the break to compliment it. The script might be used simultaneously with any of the following.

1. soft drum cadence	5. woodwinds
2. silence	6. bell lyra
3. singing	7. ensemble or section
4. whistling	8. full band (pp)

*Blessed Sacrament C.Y.O. Drum and Bugle Corps,
Newark, New Jersey
Marty Nolan and Vincent Walsh, Co-directors*

Some formations are enhanced by anticipating their music in the formation break. The music, usually played softly under a P.A. announcement, is coordinated with it so that it ends as the formation becomes legible and the music changes abruptly to full volume. It goes without saying that if the P.A. has nothing to offer, the above techniques might be used without it.

In a "theme continuity" or a performance having one basic underlying idea, it is a common practice to repeat a selection used as theme music at every break. A performance based on the theme of "work" might, for instance, use "Whistle While You Work" between each formation.

Formation breaks offer a wide area for creative thinking. They might take upon all the characteristics of a precision drill, instead of a period of chaos.

chapter V

Form

The need for form in music was felt very early in the history of music. Form aided both the composer in his expression and the listener in his comprehension. The development of form is an integral part of the evolution of music. History has treated form kindly when it served as an aid for the composer, but harshly when it became a shackle, restricting his expression.

A glance at the development of the modern halftime performance reveals form not unlike that of music, bearing the benefits and the limitations of the former. Designers of halftime performances look to form to provide the same qualities of interest, unity, and variety that has long been a part of music. Forms identifiable in the marching performance are quite akin to their counterparts in music. The theme and variations is the obvious example.

Four forms are readily discernible in the development of the marching band performance. They are:

        a. central theme continuity
        b. narative continuity
        c. potpourri continuity
        d. drill or action continuity

The first two forms are closely associated and they will be considered together. By way of definition the central theme form or continuity concerns itself with a broad theme such as: work, radio, sports, holidays, etc. The narrative form tells a story in music and motion. Favorite narrative themes are those like the homecoming story, the Legend of Paul Bunyon, Little Red Riding Hood, and historical or biographical sketches.

Both forms are obviously dependent upon a public address system. They represent the most popular type of halftime performance. As

Stan Stitgen, Wisconsin Drum Major, 1951-1955

a matter of fact, one famous marching band was recently criticized by a fan, for not having a theme in its performance.

A good theme offers a wide scope of creative thinking. It is a very valuable way to create unity. It might also be stated that a mediocre formation is certainly more acceptable when it has special meaning in a theme sequence. The choice of a good theme is of the utmost importance. Unless it is broad, allowing for a variety of possible formations, it may force the inclusion of mediocre ideas.

Many examples can be given of themes that have served as restrictions instead of aids to the director.

The potpourri style continuity has the advantage of being the least restrictive. Generally the audience feels no particular need for a theme sequence. The popular T.V. variety show is an excellent example. With only the services of a master of ceremonies to briefly set the stage, every conceivable act follows in no particular semblance of order.

The potpourri continuity might include sequences as varied as the following list:

1. precision type drill entrance
2. Liberty Bell formation for the Crusade of Freedom
3. square dance routine
4. animated formation — cowboy and lariat
5. school monogram
6. marching exit

The drill or action continuity is not dependent on a public address system. It might be described as a performance based on marching maneuvers rather than formations. Form here, is dictated by contrast, variety, and smooth flowing motion. The drum and bugle corps movement in the United States is based on this type of marching performance. It has found a great deal of favor with bands in areas where stadium seats are too low to make formations legible.

Marching Drills in Halftime Form

The emphasis of the final chapters deals with marching drills and maneuvers. It seems important, then, that their function in the halftime performance be discussed in some detail.

Drills and maneuvers, in addition to formations, comprise the bulk of activity on the halftime gridiron. The rapid development of the formation style performance has, to a great extent, by-passed the great potential of the marching drill. The action continuity, above, is an exception.

Most marching drills, well planned and thought out, are no more difficult to execute than the typical formation. The variety and interest they engender readily explains their rising popularity throughout the country. A great deal of this popularity is engendered by enthusiastic directors and bandmen who find a renewed sense of esprit de corps and pride in individual accomplishment through their use. The formation style of marching tends to de-emphasize the individual by hiding him in some design. Precision marching emancipates him and places a higher premium on individual participation and achievement.

There is a place for marching drills in every halftime performance, as indeed, there is a growing demand. A great deal has been written and recorded about every imaginable band formation, but little has been said about marching. The following chapters concern themselves not with a further listing of formations, but with actual *marching for marching bands*.

chapter VI

The Habitat

The very rapid growth of the school band movement in the United States has frequently been attributed to the versitility of the band itself. While serving as an adequate medium for music education it is still at home in the stadium, on the street, or in the town band shell. The scope of interest here, however, is confined to the gridiron, the area of the marching band's most serious concentration. The following discussion will constantly refer to yardline position, so very valuable in the stadium. It should not be assumed, however, that yardlines are a necessary prerequisite for the drills and maneuvers to follow. They might very easily be adapted to any area large enough to enclose the band.

The football field itself, is our first point of interest. It is impossible to know too much about the "habitat" in which the band will spend many hours of intensive work. The diagram below gives the measurements of the N.C.A.A. sanctioned gridiron.

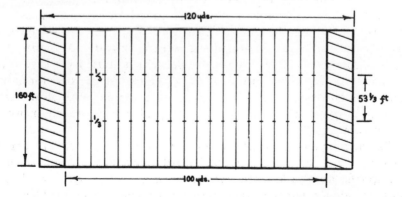

Field markings are of utmost importance to the marching band. Each individual field is worthy of concentrated study, for some contain markings not present on others. Frequently yardline numbers will be found lettered on the turf which can be of great value to the band. These numbers are usually found between the 1/3 stripes and the sidelines. As such they serve as one other means of aligning horizontal lines.

End-zone markings and designs also can be valuable to the band. They can assure precision alignment of the starting formation, with the important result of a fine first impression on the audience. Since the interval between ranks in a starting position is normally $2\frac{1}{2}$ yards or five yards the following diagrams illustrate very useful markings.

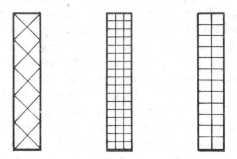

A properly marked field can save the director and the band hours of rehearsal time. Every effort to encourage the athletic department to use maximum markings will reward the director multifold.

The majority of football fields are raised in the center along a line parallel to the sidelines so that they slope to the sidelines for purposes of drainage. Formations which extend no higher than midfield then, are aligned on a slope which aids legibility. Unfortunately, this slope may work a disadvantage on formations which extend beyond the high area. In stadia with low stands this can often be a crucial problem; a problem of which many are uncognizant.

The field marking which serves as the greatest "crutch" for the marching band is, of course, the yardline mark. When a system of a specific number of steps per five yards is employed, guiding of ranks no longer remains as a major time consuming problem. As a band gets the "feel" of equal paces, rank alignment becomes automatic.

Six or eight steps per five yards are the most common units in popular usage.   In the case of six steps per five yards each step must be thirty inches long.   High school groups using the thirty inch pace usually find it too long for the high step, but very well suited to a military type pace.   More mature marching units often prefer the six-step system because of its adaptability to a military style pace.

Eight steps per five yard line necessitates a standard pace of twenty-two and one-half inches.   Getting the feel of eight equal steps per yard line is not difficult although measuring the pace in terms of a half inch seems ridiculous.   A $22\frac{1}{2}$ inch pace is very small for most marchers of any age.   A college or high school group attempting to use the military style step of only $22\frac{1}{2}$ inches presents the appearance of shuffling along, or of being held back. If the knee is lifted, however, the shorter pace presents no problem. The popularity of the high step might well be attributed, to a great extent, to this fact.   There is a natural tendency to speed up a tempo when the high step is employed.   The die is cast, then.   Natural forces have dictated the popular style of eight steps per yard line, the high step, and a more rapid tempo.   Since this system has the gross advantage of coinciding with the natural phrases of the bulk of marching music, its future popularity seems destined for a long tenure.   Realizing that the $22\frac{1}{2}$ pace has been dictated by five yard field markings, it is interesting to imagine what a different style would have been developed if the field markings were of other units.

The third stripes are undoubtedly the next most important markings to be found on the gridiron.   As the five yard lines have eliminated a great deal of rank alignment difficulty, the third stripes have reduced the difficulty of file alignment appreciably.   They locate the two outside files in down-field marching and help prevent slanting or sliding movement towards the sidelines.   The outside files are either located on the third stripes or a given distance away from them.

It would be wonderful for marching bands if the modern gridiron was ruled in squares of an earlier day.   Probably every marching director has had visions of elaborately marked fields taking the guess work out of alignment.   In lieu of this Elysian field, however, it behooves the director to encourage maximum field markings and to make maximum use of them.

chapter VII

The Small Unit Turn

It seems only logical that the basic formation of the marching band be designed for maximum maneuverability on the football field, yet the traditional block formation does not fulfill this need. The following diagram illustrates a very familiar type of marching block formation.

.   .   .   .   .   .

.   .   .   .   .   .

.   .   .   .   .   .

.   .   .   .   .   .

.   .   .   .   .   .

etc.

The formation is characterized by wide files with a comparatively small interval between ranks. The two and one half yard block between all bandsmen is a very familiar one. While it is a beautiful marching formation making maximum use of diagonals, it is not well suited for maneuvering. Actually it is quite limited in the type of maneuver that leads smoothly from it. Flanks, obliques, and to-the-rear movements are best suited. They might be executed in a large variety of units. The band might be broken into two or more sections, each pivoting in a different direction for a given number of counts before returning. Ranks, files, or combinations of each might be treated in the same manner. Alternation of pivots add another variation to the whole procedure, but it is easily seen that the scope of maneuvers possible from the block is limited in type if not in variation. If, however, the interval between ranks is enlarged the small unit turn becomes a possibility, greatly enlarging the field of maneuvering possibility. The band can now radically change its entire appearance in as few as four or eight counts by merely executing a small unit turn.

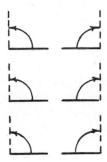

Maneuvering the band from the traditional block to a wide-interval basic formation, illustrated above, can . be executed in a variety of ways.

     a. As the band proceeds downfield in a tight block formation, the back rank might mark-time upon reaching its open alignment position. It is followed in turn by each rank in front of it. The rapid expanding effect of this simple maneuver creates an interesting effect.

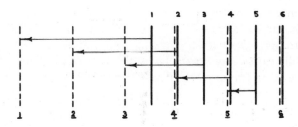

     b. The band can, if it is centered in the middle of the field, open out in both directions simultaneously in a very few number of counts. Once again the explosion effect makes this a very serviceable maneuver.

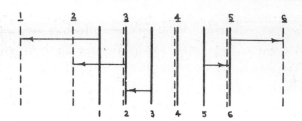

c. The formation of double ranks accomplishes the purpose of clearing out the area between the yardlines, making for added maneuverability.
d. Special entrances, illustrated in a later chapter, are excellent ways of opening up alignment.
e. Various to-the-wings type maneuvers may be utilized to set up larger fronts with the same file intervals.

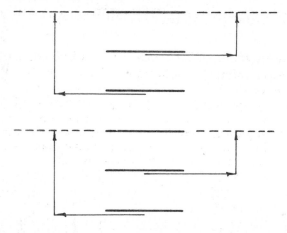

f. Many of the drills and maneuvers illustrated in Chapter IX can be utilized for this purpose.

The small unit turn makes other demands upon basic alignment. Drills are certainly more simple to execute if the number of men per rank is an even number which can be divided equally into half ranks. The second qualification is that the standard interval between men in a rank be equal, or approximately equal to the interval needed to evenly space one half of the rank between the yard lines after a turn by half ranks has been executed. The diagram below defines these intervals more clearly.

University of Wisconsin Band
Various Basic Formations

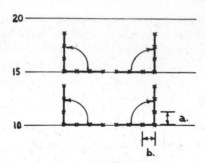

It is very feasible to open or close the interval between men in a rank while turning. The turning motion covers the adjustment, but care must be taken to keep the rank alignment accurate while turning. The illustration below shows ranks being opened and closed while turning.

When a half rank, or a full rank is spaced evenly between yard-lines, the most preferable number seems to be four or five men per yard line. Six men is the maximum and two men the minimum to describe a horizontal line. The following illustration shows all of the possibilities with the intervals necessitated by each.

The intervals listed represent the distance between the center point of one bandsman to the center of the next.

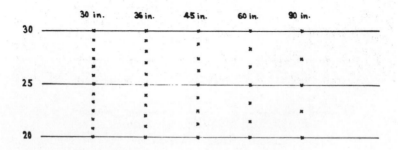

The small unit turn is usually executed in a situation where the interval between ranks allows a full turn without crowding of ranks. Because the turning rank assumes the center of attention in many drills, it is important that the turn be executed with a flourish and a unity of motion. As a result the style of pivot that turns slowly with the rank is usually preferred to the "quick pivot and wait" variety. The latter breaks up the unity of the rank and the action.

The small unit turn has many basic variations that are worthy of listing and defining. An outside-by-half-units was illustrated above in figure 1. The command for this movement is, of course, "outside by fours, etc." Outside may refer to either the sidelines or the endzones, dependent on the facing of the unit before execution. Thus:

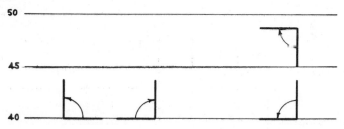

The command, "Inside by fours," would, of course, refer to the center of the playing field.

The small unit turn may take the form of a double pivot, in which case each half rank turns in a given direction at the same time.

Double Pivot Turns

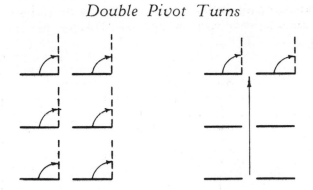

Double pivot turns may be used to turn the band 90 degrees while changing the front from full to half units. In this case it substitutes for a standard column or turning movement.

Bands which use a five or six man front can easily form a long company front by using the small unit turn. Here is a case where the interval between men has to be shortened in turning. The company front which is formed is defined as a long line or rank composed of the entire company or unit. In practical useage throughout this discussion the company front may refer to any long line, even though it often will not encompass the entire group.

On occasion, simple maneuvers like the small unit turns can be executed in succession to add momentary interest to downfield marching.

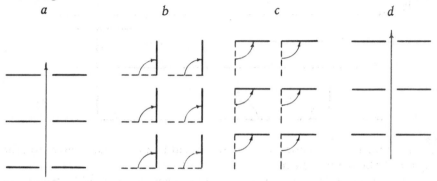

The following sequence is a variation of the same simple turn. A to-the-rear movement might follow a given number of counts of turning motion, or an entire circuit might follow. The procedure could be reversed to end up in the original position.

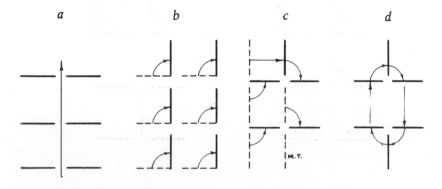

If the small unit turn is executed from longer fronts an even greater number of variations are possible. The following illustrations are executed from a twelve man front.

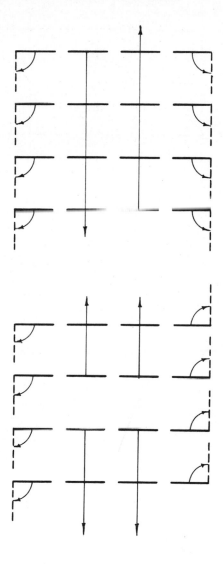

Or when broken down in three basic segments:

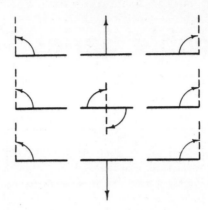

Once again the most simple way to break out of the drill situation is to reverse direction at any given point. A moments reflection will suggest an infinite number of variations which might be devised from this fundamental situation. Complex variations have been used with a good deal of success by all of the organizations which the author has directed.

The small unit turn will be recognized in many of the drills and. maneuvers which fill the final chapters.

chapter VIII

The Double Series Turn

It has been seen that small turn alignment opens up a large field of maneuvering possibility. This field can be further enlarged by a system of marching which relates turning motion to forward motion.

Unfortunately, the turn does not lend itself readily to a free interchange with forward motion. Straight motion will be defined here as forward motion, motion to the rear, flanks or obliques. All of these are executed with a full pace along a straight line. Distance, or the number of steps in a given direction can readily be ascertained with mathematical precision. Not so with the turn, for pace adjustment is mandatory in its execution. Turning motion along the circumference of a circle cannot, obviously, be executed in the same number of equal steps as can forward or straight motion.

The following illustration shows the mathematical pace requirements to complete a turn in the same number of paces as its related forward motion. The eight step per yard line system is used for illustration with a 45 inch interval (two steps) between bandsmen.

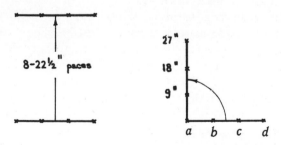

At the end of eight counts both unit #1 and unit #2 have completed their respective movements, but the pace of the outside bands-

man, letter *d*, in unit #2 had to be increased to 27 inches. Fortunately, in this case it is no more difficult to increase the pace than it
is to reduce it for the inside men. The 27 inch pace is certainly
within practical limits. Increasing the size of the basic pace is one
answer to the problem of relating the turn to forward motion.

Not all turns can be resolved so readily. If the width of the
above rank, for instance, was greatly increased, the corresponding pace
requirements of the outside man might be too long to be practical.
The following diagram shows an example of an unworkable turn.

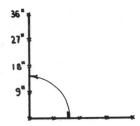

When planning a maneuver that envolves turns it is of the utmost
importance that the pace of the outside bandsman be checked, either
by pacing-off the proposed turn or mathematically. Many rehearsals
have been wasted time because a beautiful drill was based on impractical turns. In the illustration above, a 36 inch pace is impractical
for most groups. If it is executed by a mature group, some of the
effect of the turn is lost because of the hurried, awkward impression
it creates. Alignment difficulties usually increase with the length
of pace, to further complicate things.

The simple geometric formula which can be used to determine
the distance the outside man of a rank must travel in turning is, ½
the rank times pie (3.14). If a given rank, for instance, is ten feet
wide, the 90 degree arc might be found by multiplying five feet x
3.14. The answer is 15.7 feet. The size of each pace can be found
by dividing this length by the number of paces. In the case of
eight steps, each pace would be slightly less than two feet.

The diagonal turn might be utilized as a means of shortening the
outside pace. Unfortunately, the resultant distance saved is generally insignificant, yet in a few cases, it makes the difference between
possibility and impossibility. If the diagonal turn is well executed
it need not suffer visually in comparison to the wheel turn.

Since the marching illustrated here, is based on a system of pace, interval, and tempo, the basic pattern of the turn will generally be the same for any organization.   It is well to illustrate the actual pace requirements of the basic turns for a band in an early season chalk talk.   This procedure is often rewarding in helping bandsmen visualize the mechanics of the turns they must work with throughout the season.

The Simple Double Series Turn

The most basic maneuver that relates forward motion to the turn is the simple *double series turn,* illustrated below in its entirety.

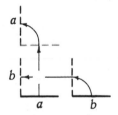

This maneuver is based on two series of equal counts.   On the first series unit *a* marches forward while unit *b* turns. (figure 1)   On the second series unit *a* turns while unit *b* marches forward in the new direction.

The double series turn can be used as a column or turn for the entire band if the interval between ranks allows for the execution of two series of counts.   From the same alignment it might also be used as an approach to a company front.

The Turn   *To a Company Front*

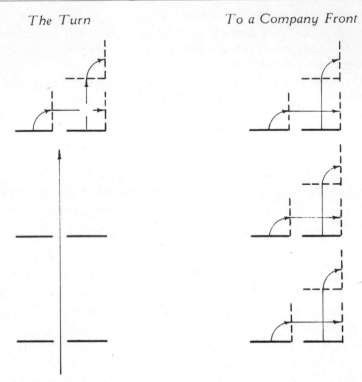

The double series turn is a fundamental movement that will be recognized in many of the drills and maneuvers to follow.

Problems of Successive Turns

There is another problem relating forward motion to the turn which can be illustrated through the double series turn. The problem, stated in rather concise terms, is as follows. A rank preceding in a given direction through a series of turns, progresses by the width of the turning rank, rather than by a full pace in that direction. Shown at the top of page 45, the turning rank actually loses one full interval each turn.

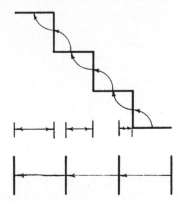

It can easily be seen that interval discrepancy increases directly with the number of turns executed in succession.

Two solutions are offered for this problem. The most simple one is to slow down the forward motion to conform with the turn. Unfortunately, the smaller pace has the effect of restraining or slowing down the action, which is avoided if at all possible. The second solution is the use of the *moving pivot*.

In the illustration above, the discrepancy in alignment would cease to exist if the pivot always advanced one pace, while turning, in the new direction. In cases of this sort where the moving pivot might be employed to good advantage, it is well to have the pivot man progress one interval in the new direction while taking the same number of steps as the outside bandsman. As in the normal pivot, the body turns slowly with the progress of the rank as a whole.

The moving pivot is a valuable aid to the band when it is capable of functioning. Its use is limited, however, by the length of the interval to be "made up." If this interval is a fairly long one it may necessitate a longer outside turning distance than practical. It obviously is of more practical value in small units than in large ones.

The double series turn presents another statement of the same problem. The following illustration pictures segments of two double series turns working toward each other. The object here, is to have each half of rank #2, shown as 2R (right half) and 2L (left half), converge and form behind rank #1 as it precedes upfield. Using standards pivots as shown, rank #2 ends up one pace behind its proper position and one pace from the center. This unhappy situation is illustrated by the dotted lines in the drawing.

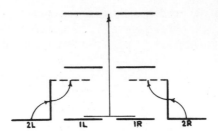

If the pivot man advanced one pace in the new direction utilizing the moving pivot the problem would be eliminated and the second rank would be properly aligned.

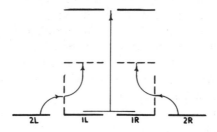

In many cases the problem created by the original turn can be erased by increasing the size pace for a series after a normal pivot has been executed. The drawings below illustrate both the moving pivot and the increased pace applied to a turn followed by forward motion.

Moving Pivot   *Lengthened Pace*

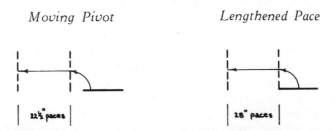

It is felt that the reader should be cognizant of the problems of turning motion vs. forward motion. In actual practice many groups have executed maneuvers of this type without being aware of the minor discrepancies that do exist. The marcher involuntarily adjusts to the situation. Because the double series turn and most of the drills illustrated are based on series of steps the goal of each series is easily comprehended. It might be necessary to make minor adjustments within a series of steps, but the series themselves are treated mathematically so that turning motion does, in reality, correspond to forward motion.

Charting of motion is normally confined to the definition of series of steps. The problems discussed in this chapter might be solved in any of the ways suggested depending on the individual situation. It is important that the director is able to specify what technique, if any, is to be used. In the charts of the maneuvers to follow the moving pivot, or the need for advancing one interval will be illustrated as in example *a*. The stationary, or the normal pivot is shown in figure *b*.

a   *b*

The Turn At Six Steps Per Five Yardline

The simple turn and the double series turn is somewhat more complicated to execute by a band marching six steps per yard line. Since the basic pace is 30 inches long, it cannot be lengthened a great deal for turning motion. The width of the turning rank assumes a greater importance here, for it must allow the outside bandsman to complete the turn in six counts. Normally a band marching a six man front and turning by half ranks does not find this difficult.

Larger bands, however, may find it necessary to shift into eight steps per yard line as a special drill pace. The shift has the disadvantage of changing the size of the standard pace which may lead to momentary confusion. As described above though, the series system in effect here, makes the goal easy to visualize and adjustment quite simple. The University of Wisconsin Band for a number of seasons used a system of six steps per yard line, shifting into eight steps for drill purposes.

Ranks of Odd Numbers

It was stated earlier in this discussion that an even number of men per rank is best suited for the system of marching under discussion. While this remains true, it is possible for a band preferring to march five or seven men abreast to shift through a neutral position into an even numbered rank for drill purposes. The illustration below, shows a rank of five men realigning itself in a six man front.

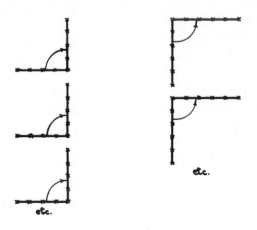

Center Wheels

The center wheel is a type of turn that lends itself equally well to large or small units. It is valuable both as an interesting maneuver in itself or as a functional means of fitting many maneuvers together.

In even numbered ranks there is no bandsman on the true center of the rank. The center is found half way between the innermost bandsmen. It is on this point that the wheel revolves.

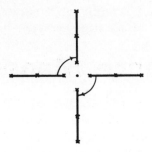

The center wheel might be executed in two basic ways.

    a. Half of the rank, the right half as shown in the illustra-
        tion, might execute a to-the-rear or an about face and
        step off in the new direction, or:
    b. The right half of the rank might march backwards in
        a turning motion.

The latter technique is generally preferred. It is not difficult to
execute and it has a startling effect. The wheel can revolve in either
direction, but it is well to standardize a definite direction. A simple
rule might be: "the right half of a rank always marches backward
.in a clockwise direction, the left half moves forward and clockwise."

chapter IX

Entrance Maneuvers

Perhaps no segment of the halftime performance is of more importance than the entrance. The axiom concerning the value of the first impression certainly extends to the gridiron. Many organizations, for instance, feeling that a faster-than-normal cadence creates a good first impression, enter rapidly and then purposefully let the tempo lag to a more practical tempo. The subtle change in cadence may be obvious to the musician, but seldom does the spectator realize that the band does not continue to march rapidly throughout its entire performance.

Tempo, however, is just one element that the director might consider to be of importance in creating a first impression. Fanfares, music, marching, novel starting positions, or any number of other techniques might be employed to accomplish the same purpose. Certainly the first impression of the music heard on the field is extremely important. Marching itself, assumes its most universal importance in the entrance, for there is no other legitimate way to get a band to the center of the field! Even organizations that run from formation to formation with a minimum of marching are forced to march on and off. It is not impossible, however, to see an organization actually run, every man for himself, to the first formation from the sidelines. Using this technique, it has been demonstrated, all to often, how a band can fill up a halftime performance without marching a step as a unit.

It is the purpose of this chapter to present various maneuvers which may be of value in enlarging the scope of traditional band entrances. The maneuvers diagramed illustrate types, or basic movements which can readily be revised to fit any size organization. It is also desired that they will suggest to the reader other maneuvers based on the same principles envolved.

If we can point to any entrance formation and call it traditional, it would certainly be the block entrance. The marching block is probably the finest formation ever devised for the marching band. Few formations can match the appeal of a band passing by with straight ranks, files, and diagonals. It seems highly desirable to include a marching block somewhere in every game performance, but it is probably not remiss to say that the block is usually best suited to a segment of the performance other than the halftime entrance.

The widespread formation from sideline to sideline has won great favor as a starting position because of its wide scope of maneuvering possibility. This type of entrance can, of course, be executed from either endzone, sideline, or perhaps a combination of two or more locations. It is these widespread or "company front" entrances that absorb the attention of this chapter.

The Marching Company Front

The sight of a band lined up from sideline to sideline ready to begin a halftime performance more than likely suggests marching the front straight ahead. As the steps per yardline system of alignment gained in popularity, parading the field in a company front also became popular. When a bandsman has grasped the relationship of pace to the yardlines, the company front is technically no more difficult to execute than the marching block. Indeed, if diagonals are emphasized in the block formation, the company front is the more simple to execute.

A marching company front is a thrilling movement to see. Perhaps, it still reminds us of the charge of the Light Brigade or the battle lines of a more colorful era. A high premium is placed upon a straight rank. While the maneuver has no files or diagonals to serve as pitfalls, a slight error in rank alignment is easily noticed. For this reason, it is well for a group to have attained a substantial degree of proficiency before the marching front is attempted.

Marching company fronts are not hazardous if they move for shorter distances. Forward motion, for as little as eight or sixteen steps is very effective and yet, not risky. Should minor problems of alignment occur, they will probably not be observed by the bulk of the audience that sees the front marching toward it.

Sooner or later the company front must be broken down into smaller marching units, or perhaps the first formation. The "break-

down" to smaller marching units, or a block formation, is the basis
of many maneuvers described below. It matters little if they are
called entrances, drills, maneuvers, or basic techniques, for in reality,
they are all of these things.

Echelon Entrances

A company front starting position is an ideal alignment from
which echelon patterns may be formed. Moving echelons, majestic
and complex looking, are comparatively simple to execute. Unlike
the company front, where error seems magnified, the echelon hides
error because of the increased visual span and the smaller units. The
figure below illustrates a simple, yet effective, way to form a wedge
type echelon from a company front.

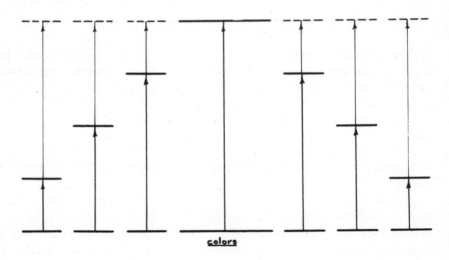

colors

In this case the echelon is accomplished by a series of counts, relative to the number of ranks used. Six series are used in the above
illustration to actually form the echelon. On series one, the first
eight counts probably, the lead or center rank steps off. In this case,
the color guard has replaced the first rank as the center group. All
other ranks mark time on the first series. On the second series the
middle ranks adjacent to the colors step off while the colors continue
upfield and the other ranks continue to mark time until their turn
arrives. This process is continued until the echelon is completely

formed. The echelon may then continue down-field in formation as long as desired.

The most simple way to break the echelon is to reform the company front in the center of the field. In this case the lead rank marks time on a given yard-line and waits until the other ranks form on its flanks. Small bands may then break from the company front by executing a right turn by ranks. If this movement was desired, the ranks would have been realigned on the starting line so that they would be in their proper order after the turn is completed. The double series turn described in Chapter VIII could easily be substituted for the simple turn in the above movement, if desired. The completed turn brings a small band to the sidelines, in a position best suited for its ensuing sequences. This turn breakdown would not be executed with the colors in the center. A rank would be substituted for the colors.

When a color guard is used as the lead rank a center breakdown is required so that the colors continue to lead the band. This type of breakdown is shown below. Obviously, this maneuver could be used from the starting line without the echelon movement preceding it.

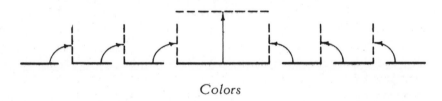

Colors

It is, by no means, necessary to reform a company front before breaking down an echelon formation. By merely executing an inside turn after the echelon has been formed, it is a simple process to set up two lines through which the colors or some featured section might pass in review.

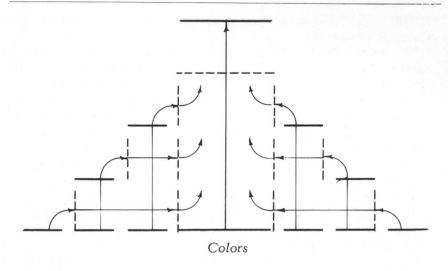

Colors

A most stirring and respectful presentation of the national colors can be staged in this manner. The picture presented by the band in parallel fronts, serving as an honor guard, through which the colors pass in review is a spectacular one. Such a presentation has become a tradition of the pre-game performance of the University of Wisconsin Marching Band. The colors of the four services of our nation's armed forces pass through four separate lanes, mass, and precede upfield through the band. 55,000 people rise to attention as they pass by to the strains of , "You're a Grand Old Flag."

After the colors have passed through the lanes in the above diagram, all ranks turn into the alley simultaneously. They are automatically aligned at five yard intervals. Larger bands marching six abreast, might easily adapt this maneuver so that the band will reform at $2\frac{1}{2}$ yard intervals by shortening the interval between men in the starting position, so in turning, six men are spaced between the yardlines instead of three. In the final upfield turn the ranks will now be spaced at $2\frac{1}{2}$ yard intervals. The latter procedure is shown in the illustration at top of page 55.

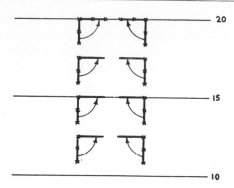

An interesting variation of the above maneuver is shown below. In this illustration the ranks are renumbered on the starting line. As the colors pass by, in the same manner described above, the band forms to their rear, rank by rank, in eight count series. When completely formed the band is following the colors upfield at five yard intervals.

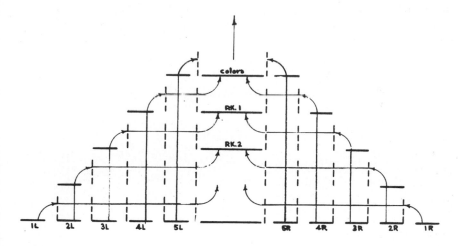

A reverse echelon is formed by stepping off from the outsides and progressing inward, as shown below. A very pleasing variation of the colors presentation shown above can be achieved by having the colors step off as the reverse echelon ranks pivot to the center and proceed into lanes. The angle of the open echelon after the turn

allows the bulk of the stadium to see the colors step off.   As the
colors proceed upfield, the lanes closing in from the two flanks make
a most pleasing picture of color, motion, and symmetry.

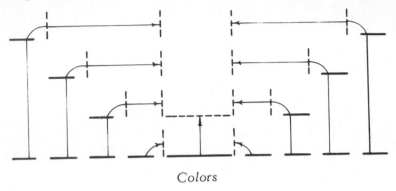

Colors

The following illustration looks identical to one seen previously
in this chapter.   When it is executed according to the instruction
below, however, it bears little resemblence to the former.   In this
illustration the entire company front steps off together.   In suc-
ceeding series, corresponding half ranks turn inside, starting from
the outside and working towards the center.   Only the initial and
the final positions are the same in both maneuvers.   The latter maneuver has the effect of a company front moving upfield.   This effect
can be extended by delaying the turning movement.   As the turning motion begins the company front gradually becomes shorter while
the new ranks moving toward the center of the field become gradually longer.

The halftime entrance of the University of Wisconsin Band at
the Rose Bowl was a complicated combination of three entrances
used previously throughout the season.   The next Figure illustrates
a portion of this entrance.   It is inserted here to illustrate how the
basic movements presented up to this point can be adapted to bands
which are too large to form one company front.

Figure *a* presents the original placement of the ranks, or half ranks.
The music used was the famous, "Saint Louie Blues March," which
has since become a favorite with bands throughout the country.
After the introduction, the entire band stepped off in its original
alignment.   In alternate series, marked for each unit, the units "froze"
with one foot forward and one back.   After a short drum interlude

with the band standing motionless, it again stepped off as one unit and proceeded upfield to the company fronts shown in figure *b*.

Figure *c* illustrates the breakdown of the three company fronts. It will be noted that the second and third rank mark time for two series after the rank in front starts its breakdown. As the individual ranks reform they move directly into double ranks, although, they could have formed at any interval.

Here is a case where the delay of movement helps to sustain interest. It would not be necessary to execute the break of the fronts in this manner if the delay seemed undesirable. The breakdown could be executed by readjusting the original placement of the ranks and by turning the ranks in alternate directions into the block formation. In this way the gap between the three fronts can be filled quickly and symmetrically.

Figure *a*

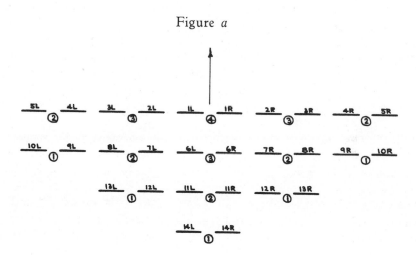

Figure *b*

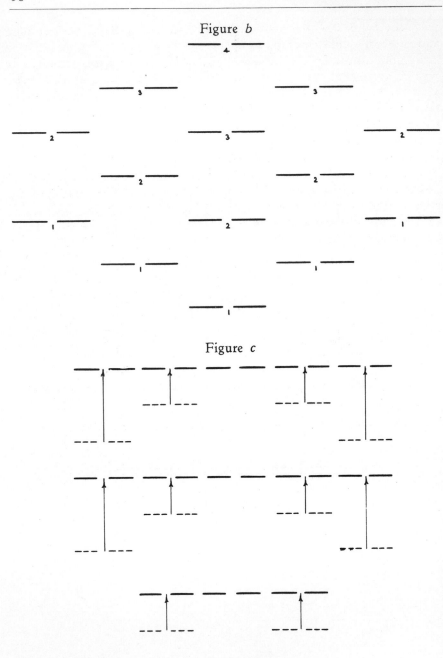

Figure *c*

Figure *d*

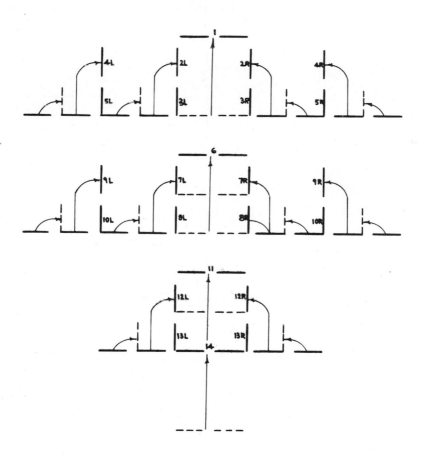

Figure *e*

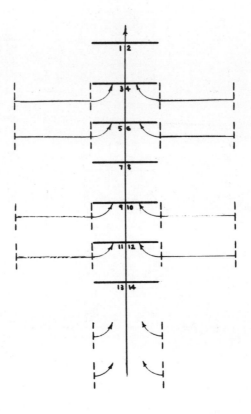

University of Wisconsin Band

Multiple Turn Entrance

Figure 1 on page 62, illustrates a type of echelon maneuver based on a series of small unit turns. Starting from a company front, each rank turns continuously back and forth until two lanes have been completely formed. At this point the lanes might be treated in the manner described previously or they might move upfield immediately, ignoring the lane idea.

Figure 1

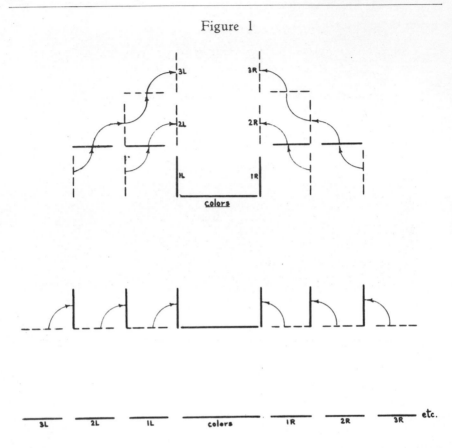

Figure 2 shows a variation of this maneuver where the colors are not shown as the center unit, and where the lane effect is not established. Rank 1 precedes directly upfield followed by each other forming rank. The marching block established will be spaced at five yard intervals.

Figure 2

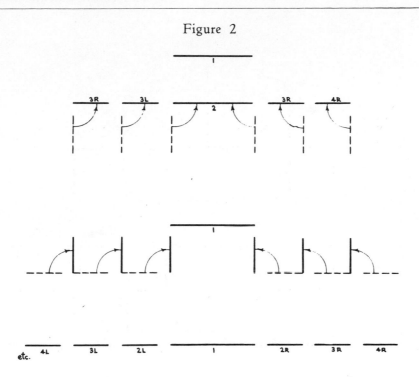

Either of these maneuvers could incorporate the use of the double series turn. Figure 3, for instance, is the counterpart of Figure 2 utilizing the double series turn.

Figure 3

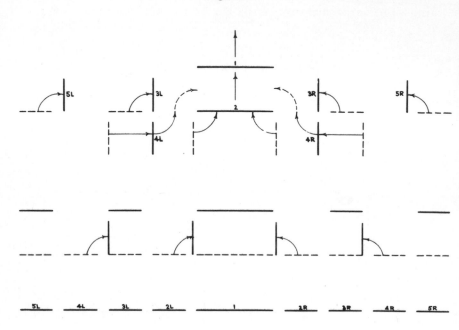

In compiling material for this chapter a number of sequences were taken out of larger maneuvers performed by one of the organizations with which the author has worked. They were selected to illustrate some feature of the precision style of marching dealt with in this discussion. In the search for clarity, subtle changes have often been made in the original maneuver. It is, however, a most intriguing feature of this style of marching that a subtle change often changes the entire effect of a maneuver. The following diagram shows a maneuver which owes its existence to such a circumstance. The reader may see a relationship in the basic technique used in other drills, but the result is quite unique. Actually this maneuver has not as yet been executed.

Once again for the sake of clarity a small unit has been used for illustration purposes, but there is no limitation imposed for its successful execution. In larger groups the action shown in the fifth series would be delayed until all ranks are in position for the inside turn. The entire maneuver is shown below in Figure 4.

Figure 4

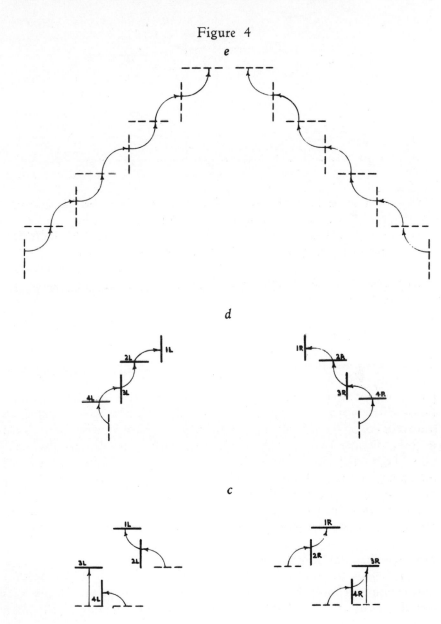

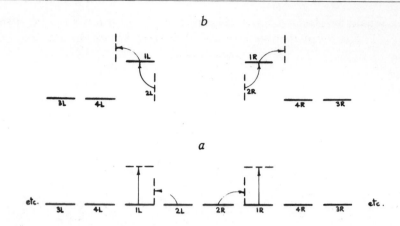

Many entrances have the effect of breaking down the band from a widespread formation to a marching block in the same length of time necessary to march a block straight forward. Figure 5 illustrates a novel entrance which marches the band through itself into a block without a loss of forward motion. This formation was originally used to present U. W. drum-major Stan Stitgen at the first game of the football season.

Figure 5

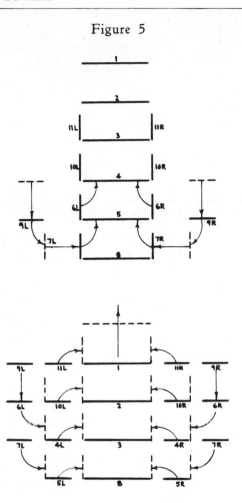

In adapting the above maneuver for varying sized organizations, the basic action remains the same, but changes will undoubtedly be required in the starting alignment and in the sequences to follow. Figure 6 illustrates how it might be adapted for a smaller band of nine ranks.

Figure 6

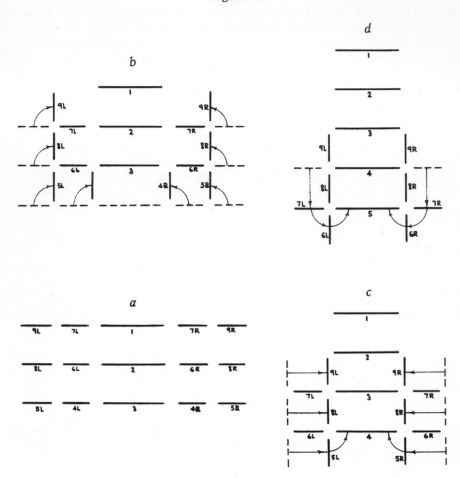

File Entrances

All of the entrances or maneuvers illustrated thus far have been based on the basic motion or manipulation of ranks. File maneuvers offer a welcome variation to this general pattern. File entrances have particular value in evolving more tightly aligned block formations from widespread starting positions.

Figures 7-8-9 can be discussed as a group since they are all different applications of the same maneuver. The file entrance is based on two simple requirements.   The rank and file interval between all bandsmen in the starting position must be equal and the files must be aligned in such a way that they can unwind without crossing, marking time, or half stepping.   The idea is so simple it seems impossible that the final result is as startling and interesting to watch.

Figure 7

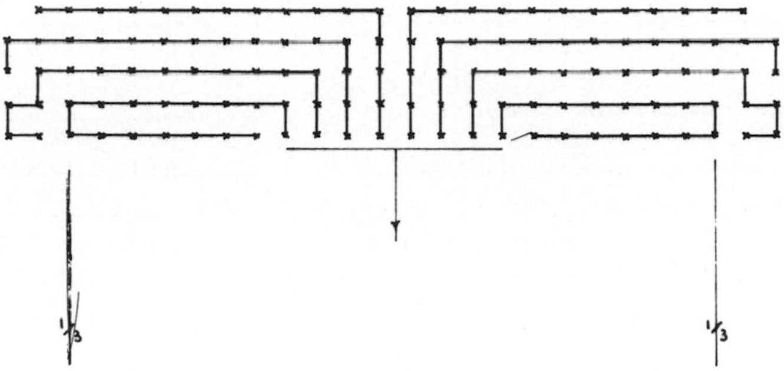

Figure 8

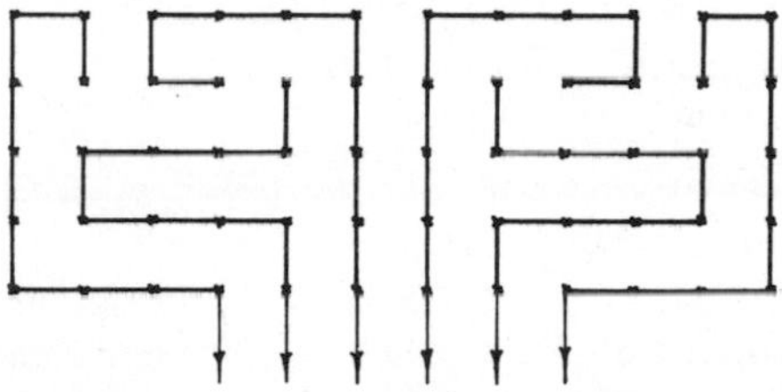

Figure 9

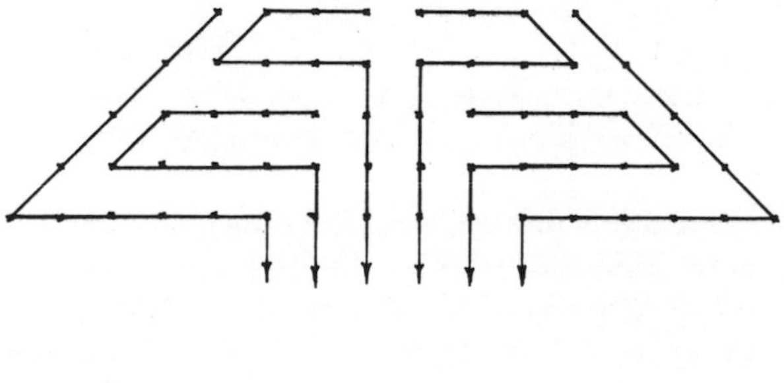

chapter X

Progressive
File Maneuvers

In the quest of originality and novelty, hours too often fly by while the harrassed director lashes little dots across an innocent sheet of paper already tortured by the persistent carresses of an overpassionate eraser. The Goddess of novelty exacts an exhausting tribute for her fleeting favors. Like the sirens of a legendary day, she charms us away from the simple and the obvious into the labyrinth of the impossible.

Novelty need not infer the difficult. A study of the most simple fundamentals of marching may reveal a freshness as yet undiscovered. Someone turned such a soulsearching glance at the simple flank countermarch and discovered the progressive pivot countermarch. Figure 1 illustrates the progressive pivot applied to the double-flank type countermarch. For the sake of simplicity, a very small group is utilized. The interval between files is two paces and the rank interval is four paces. The latter is very important since it controls the "staggered interval."

On command or cue, the right guide of the first rank executes two right flanks followed in turn, by each bandsman to his left at two count intervals. As each bandsman completes his pivots he becomes a part of a new partial or full rank. When this initial part of the maneuver is completed, the files are staggered at four pace intervals between men. See Figure 1 c.

In this staggered formation the band is aligned in a refreshing alignment which might suggest many novel sequences. Figure 1d illustrates one way to reform a traditional front. In this case the original right guide again executes two right flanks, followed in two count series by his rank-mates. As each completes his pivots the rank automatically reforms in its original alignment.

Figure 1

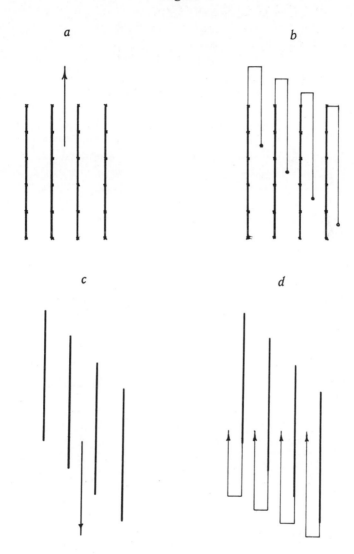

Small bands that find the turn an acceptable maneuver on the football field, may execute a novel and interesting turn from the staggered formation mentioned above. Figure 2 illustrates this turn. On cue or command the right guide executes a right flank followed at two count intervals by his rank-mates. (note: it is the original right guide that turns first, not the right guide of the staggered alignment.)   As each bandsman turns he becomes a part of the forming rank aligned in the original position.

This maneuver is well suited to the street parade: particularly, the slow moving one that allows time to "set-up" the turn.   The set-up procedure is illustrated in Figures 1a-1b-1c.   A moments reflection will suggest to the reader other more simple procedures of alignment if they seem desirable.   In executing this type of file maneuver it is only necessary that the front rank understand the exact procedure.   All other members of the file merely execute the maneuver preformed by the man in front of him at the point where he executed it.

Figure 2

From this simple treatment of the staggered position turn a more involved maneuver leads easily.   It is obvious, of course, that the staggered turn and its set-up can be executed in either direction. The new maneuver is based on a staggered turn in opposite directions simultaneously.   It is shown in Figure 3.

Figure 3

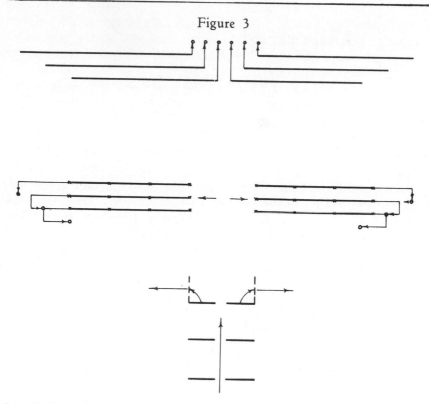

As the two sections approach each other, aligned in the staggered formations, the lead men pivot upfield when they reach their normal position. In a situation of this kind the cross pivot may be used to allow pivots in opposite directions simultaneously. The standard army pivot executed on alternate counts is quite possible, however. A later chapter discusses these pivots in more detail. When this maneuver is well executed it is most pleasant to watch.

The entire sequence could be executed from a company front with excellent results. Figure 4 suggests an outside by 3's or half units. This alignment can then be easily converted into the staggered formation as shown above.

Figure 4

chapter XI

Minstrel
Turn Maneuvers

The minstrel show of a more gay and colorful decade has enriched both Webster's dictionary and the vocabulary of the American heart. Even the modern marching band is indebted to the "burnt cork" artists for at least one of its most familiar terms, "the minstrel turn." It is not inconceivable that the minstrel's art has contributed a great deal more to the heritage of the marching band than historians have yet discovered.

Figure 1 helps to define the term which was frequently a part of minstrel dance routines.

Figure 1

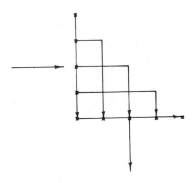

The turn has found varied favor in marching circles. In the area of drum and bugle corps and drill teams, it is very popular, while in the field of larger bands it has gained less favor because of the difficulty of executing it from the smaller intervals necessary in large groups. It is certainly best adapted to a group marching in open alignment, or with intervals between ranks equal to rank width.

Size does not, however, eliminate the minstrel turn from the practical vocabulary of the marching band. While it is difficult to execute in a block formation it may easily be adapted to widespread formations. In these open formations the basic turn takes on a new flourish and effectiveness. Figure 2 illustrates the minstrel turn executed from a company front. In this case the company front forms two fronts moving towards the center of the field. They pass and reform the original front as shown in the arrows. The diagrams fail to give the effect of the two ever growing lines proceeding towards each other while the large company front grows progressively smaller. The effect of evolving design serves well to typify the objective of precision marching.

Figure 2

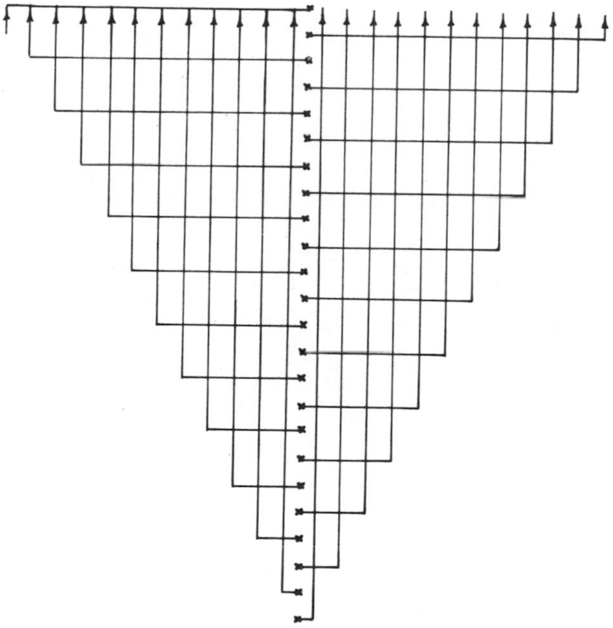

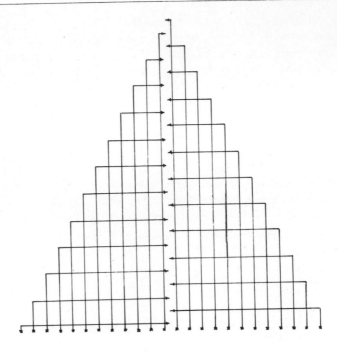

Used as a means of breaking-down a company front into a marching block, the minstrel turn is equally effective. Figure 3 indicates how the passing ranks might break into ranks of any pre-determined and pre-aligned width and interval.

Figure 3

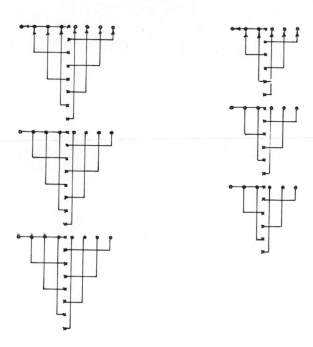

Care must be taken in the matter of pivots used in reforming after the ranks have passed through each other. The cross-over or the whirl pivot is ideally suited to the mathematical precision called for in this type of maneuver. Effort spent in perfecting the whirl pivot for use here will be most rewarding in terms of audience response.

chapter XII

File Maneuvers

In a previous chapter the merits and the limitations of the marching block formation were discussed in some detail. It was noted that to-the-wings type maneuvers were perhaps, best suited to its alignment characteristics. Manipulation of files in the tradition of the familiar army "files to-the-rear in alternate four counts" maneuver, is another type of movement which leads easily from the standard block.

The maneuvers to be presented next are nothing more than a glorification of these basic file maneuvers. Figure 1 below, illus-

Figure 1

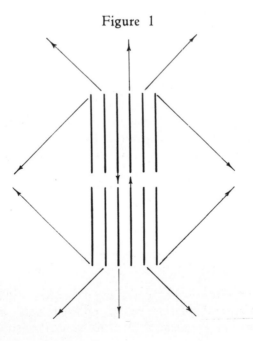

trates a file maneuver which achieves a great deal of success in the original purpose of spreading out the band, destroying the feel-ing·of the block formation.

On cue or signal, each file or half file steps off in the direction indicated by the arrow. At the end of a prescribed number of counts all segments execute some form of the to-the-rear movement and return to their original positions. The movement could be made more complex, if desired, through the addition of turns, trick. steps, or dance routines. The various facings and the spread out align-ment lends emphasis to these movements.

There is no reason why the above maneuver cannot be executed with full files moving foward in directions defined by the front rank. This method can be easily converted into an effective counter-march by merely substituting a two flank countermarch instead of the to-the-rear when the files are at their outermost point. Figure 2 diagrams this movement.

Figure 2

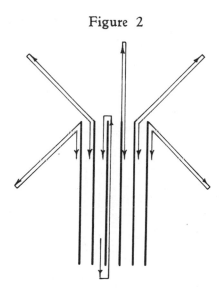

The Perpetual Motion Drill

Perhaps every director has experienced restless nights, nightmares of marching feet and blaring brass, relieved now and then with eloquent visions of bandsmen dancing merrily through routines.

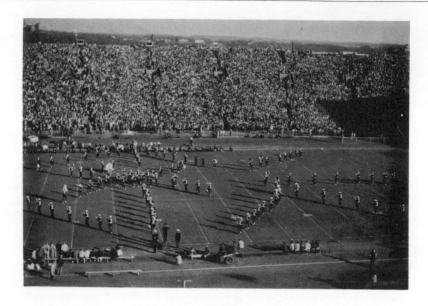

University of Wisconsin Band

Morning, and the ensuing days drill, however, give eloquent testi-
mony to the fact that the dreams of the night were dreams indeed.

Dreams are fantasies in which sousaphone players encounter no
difficulty in turning backward sommersaults without missing a note
of the, "Stars and Stripes Forever." It seems possible that the "perpetual motion" drill, with its constant motion in opposite directions
owes its existence to the routines of the little men who aren't there.

The perpetual motion drill, which received its name strictly by
default, is not a file maneuver in the strictest sense of the word. It is
included here because the files actually move upfield during the maneuver. The accompanying figures, numbers 3a-3b-etc., do not ade-
quately express the effect of the completed movement because a small
unit was chosen for purposes of illustration. Where more ranks
are used the motion to the rear is more clearly defined. Multiple
ranks actually move in both directions while the entire unit progresses up the field.

The number of series necessary to re-align the unit in its original
order is, of course, dependent on the number of ranks used in the
drill. An interesting variation of this maneuver can be brought about

Figure 3

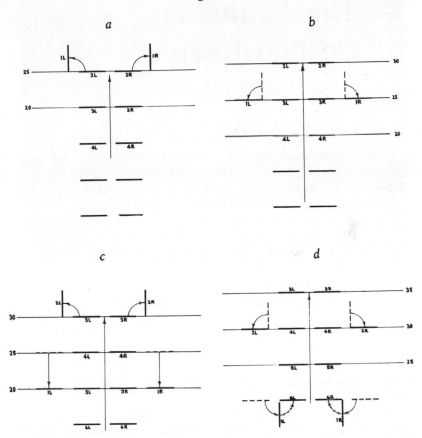

by first executing a complete outside turn by half ranks. When the perpetual motion sequences are executed from this position the effect is one of movement turning inward instead of outward.

The maneuver has the practical value of moving the band in a given direction without upsetting the alignment.

The Formation
Of Pinwheels

Few formations offer as many opportunities for interesting and varied maneuvers as does the basic pinwheel. Chapter XIII deals with methods of forming the pinwheel in various shapes and forms. Effort has been made to illustrate this section in terms of varied size groups to emphasize that there is no group for which the pinwheel cannot be adapted. Unfortunately the drills often seem hopelessly complex on paper, but the most immature group will be amazed at the rapidity with which they might be executed on the field. Once again the answer lies in the fact that the drills are complex, but they really represent a complexity of simple movements. The individual bandsman has little difficulty grasping his part of the movement. The action from the spectator's standpoint, however, is a complex picture of ever changing design, composed of motion in every conceivable direction. Somehow, when collision seems unavoidable, units of bandsmen pass within inches of each other without hesitation or side stepping.

There seems to be a way to form a pinwheel for every possible situation. One of the most simple to grasp is the method shown in Figure 1.

Half stepping might be necessary in forming the above pinwheel if the interval between ranks is too small. This can be avoided, however, if the movement starts from a stationary position and the ranks step off at definite intervals. The number of counts delayed is, of course, dependent on the time needed to turn 90 degrees.

If an organization has four or a multiple of four ranks the above method works out well. The question of what to do if the group does not conform to these number requirements is worthy of discussion. Actually an extra rank might easily be located in a straight line between two or more pinwheels. Two ranks are enough to

Figure 1

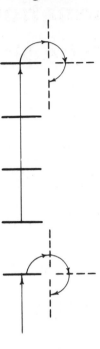

form a smaller pinwheel which can execute the same movements as the larger ones. Often the addition of these "extra" ranks serve to enhance the total movement. Frequently a solo group is picked as the extra rank which is located in a prominent position. On one occasion a group of trumpeters of the Madison Edgewood High School Band were selected to perform a popular trumpet quartet which was performed previously in concert. While they played from a stationary position the pinwheels formed and executed a percision maneuver about them. The effect was one of relief from the full sound of the entire band, while the bandsmen were free to concentrate on their marching route. Figure 2 shows the formation of pinwheels utilizing two extra ranks. Figure 2 also illustrates the method of forming multiple pinwheels from half ranks instead of full ones shown in Figure 1.

Figure 2

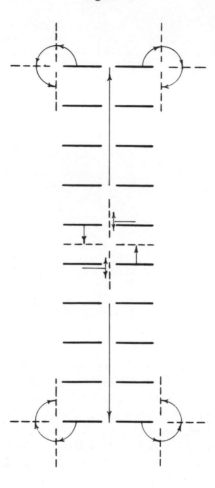

Figure 3 illustrates how pinwheels might readily be formed from double ranks aligned 10 yards apart. This is the normal interval if the double ranks were originally formed from five yard intervals. When formed with the half ranks evenly spaced between the yard-lines the pinwheels join to form a long horizontal line the length of the band. Smaller groups maneuvering near the sidelines might well make use of the third stripe to aid alignment.

Figure 3

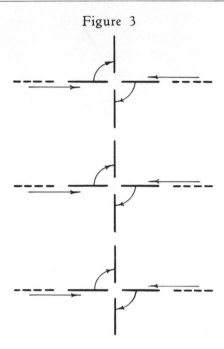

Figure 4 shows a pinwheel formed through the use of an underlying formation, in this case an open square. The conversion of
the squares into crosses in only eight counts, through the use of
center wheels is an intriguing movement to see.

Figure 4

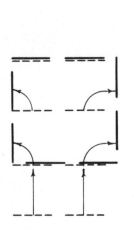 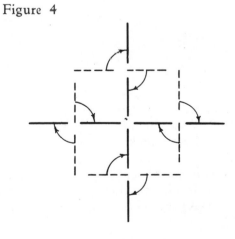

Company fronts lend themselves readily to pinwheel formations. Figure 5 illustrates one method of forming them from a company front.   Figure 6 illustrates the procedure useable when two company fronts are available.

Figure 5

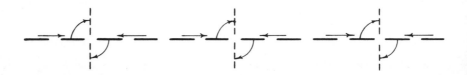

Figure 6

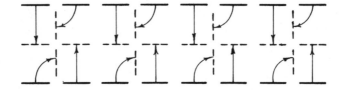

chapter XIV

Pinwheel Maneuvers

The object of any pinwheel, be it a fireworks display or a child's toy, is to spin around. It is not surprising that the basic movement of the pinwheel formed by the band is the same. Where multiple wheels are formed, they may spin together, in opposite directions or intermeshed. Larger wheels might break into two segments and revolve in opposite directions. See Figure 1 below.

Figure 1

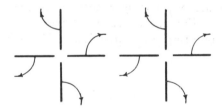

The pivot point of the ranks might be shifted to the outside bandsman with the startling change of symmetric pattern shown in Figure 2.

Figure 2

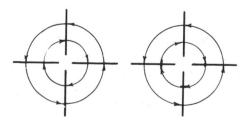

Figure 3 illustrates how a subtle change in alignment and a reversal of direction can completely alter the effect of the turning motion.

Figure 3

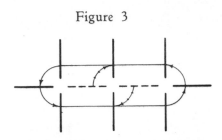

Each wing of the pinwheel can march off independently in four different directions, for the sake of convenience say 16 counts; execute a to-the-rear, return to the original position where the ranks are inches apart, and pass for another 16 counts in the new direction before returning. The point of passing the original position is a thrilling experience for the bandsman and the audience alike, yet, the maneuver is basically so simple that it has been executed by a blindfolded group. This sequence is shown in its original position with arrows pointing out direction. Variations are given in Figures 4-5-6.

Figure 4   Figure 5   Figure 6

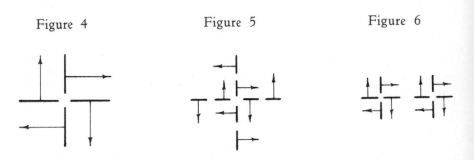

The number of drills and maneuvers based on pinwheels seem infinite. In its extended position the units can be manipulated freely. Figure 8 illustrates a more complex treatment of a pinwheel maneuver. To aid both the reader and the drillmaster in explaining the maneuver to a group, the instructions are listed in their series order.

Figure 7

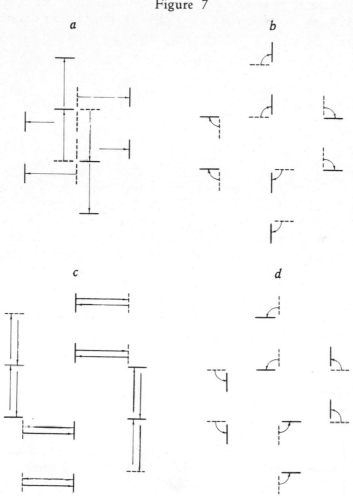

All Ranks

Series 1- out, in the given direction
Series 2- continue out
Series 3- right turn
Series 4- ahead
Series 5- to-the-rear and back
Series 6- in, towards original position
Series 7- in, to position

University of Wisconsin Band

The above maneuver can easily be extended with fine effect, by continuing on through in the new direction repeating the same eight series.

The above sequence lends itself to P.A. instruction. The drillmaster might easily give instructions for each series to be executed over the P.A. After this series is completed in eight counts, instructions for the next series is given. If all ranks are facing correctly to begin with, no difficulty will be encountered in execution. Multiple turns, freezes, delayed steps, or trick routines could be added to the sequence as outlined above if further effect is desired.

Pinwheel maneuvers offer a grand source of material for creative thinking. They apply equally well to large and small groups. On one occasion the University of Wisconsin Band was spread out over the entire playing field, with men in both endzones and across both sidelines simultaneously. The audience viewed an evolving pattern of marching men wherever it wished to look.

Figure 4 of Chapter XIII illustrated how a pinwheel could be formed from the open square. This simple maneuver of one design changing into another in a short sequence is the basis for a very interesting drill.

Figure 8 diagrams a series of designs that alternate back and forth through ever changing ranks. The eye is intrigued by the rapid change of design. Perhaps it presents the challenge of a riddle to the viewer. At any rate it is a very effective maneuver.

Figure 8

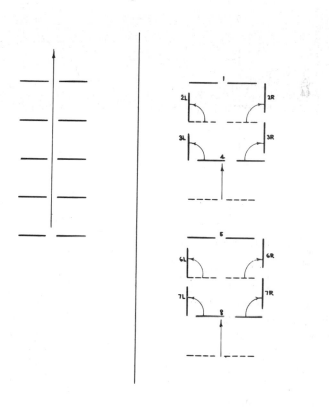

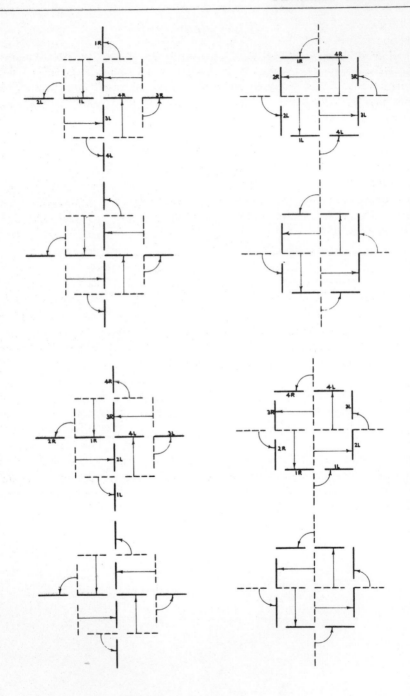

The Silent Drill

It would be a case of gross negligence to close this section on the pinwheel maneuver without a discussion of the silent drill. Where formations, drills, dances, fireworks, hand springs, and talking walrus have failed to warm the indifference of the "rooters" of a loosing team, the silent drill never fails.

The silent drill is nothing more than a sharp interruption of a sequence, where the music cuts out and each bandsman marches independently off in a direction known only to him and his nervous director. Without a signal he executes a to-the-rear and returns to his original position, miraculously bursting into sound and order from silence and chaos. The silent drill is easy to execute. It has no ranks or files, no guiding, and no music. If a bandsman gets lost it doesn't particularly matter if he keeps out of the way and gets back on time. The silent drill is a pleasure to teach!

Lest it prematurely be proclaimed as the director's "emancipation proclamation" it is well to look more closely at its technical aspects. The drill is based on the individuals ability to count carefully and to hold a given tempo for a short period of time. It is well to attempt only short sequences while the idea is still novel, however, mature groups have executed 32 or more counts accurately.

A necessary pre-requisite for the silent drill is an underlying formation that allows ample maneuvering space. The extended positions of the pinwheel maneuvers discussed in this chapter are ideal. Figure 9 illustrates a simple pattern in which the silent drill might progress. Each unit of the extended pin-wheel executes the maneuver shown in Figure 9 simultaneously. If only a nominal amount of care is taken, collisions can be avoided in diagraming. Actually the possible combinations of direction are so numerous that they seldom have to be revised.

Figure 9

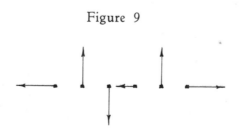

The silent drill is simple and effective. It is, however, a drill which might be classified as a gimmic. It can normally be used only sparingly in a season. Used sparingly it may serve well to direct attention at a time when the "meat" of a performance might otherwise need tenderizing.

Stationary
Formation Charts

New marching band techniques evolve rapidly, usually in the direction of the complex. This complexity, however, has as its objective its antithesis; simplicity. The planning technique on the part of the director, for instance, might well become more complex so that its execution by the band will become more simple and precise.

In the early days of the marching band, before directors had yet become conscious of using yardlines for guiding, or before they were overly concerned with the details of charting the reverse was perhaps true. Complex execution problems were born of too simple planning. Anyone who has been a part of a marching band, past or present, will agree that one of the most difficult tasks of a marching band is to march with straight ranks and files without the use of yardlines as a guide. The pace per yardline system has made charting more complex, but it has certainly simplified the work of the marching band.

Chapter XV deals with the problem of charting stationary formations. It envolves a rather detailed discussion of these problems, but once again the objective of this "envolvement" is a better and more simple way to chart formations.

Vertical versus Horizontal Interval

Perspective is a problem of a stationary design. The height of a bandsman and the distance of the formation to the audience tends to visually shorten the length of vertical intervals. Horizontal intervals (parallel to sideline) are on the other hand little effected. This situation is illustrated in the following sketches.

As Charted   *As It Appears*

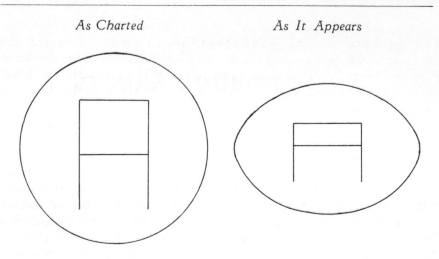

Charles Righter, State University of Iowa, used concentric squares in his book, "Gridiron Pageantry," to illustrate the same problem. The result is sketched below.

As Charted   *As It Appears*

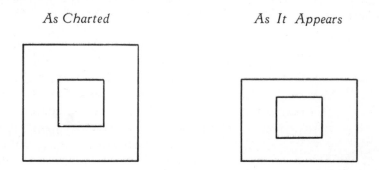

Elongation is best accomplished through a system of set proportions. A horizontal interval of 45 inches, for instance, might equal a vertical interval of 60 inches. The first step in devising an elongation system is the determination of a standard horizontal interval to be used. The vertical interval is dependent upon it.

If three men are equally spaced between two yardlines to form a horizontal line, it was seen in Chapter VII that the interval between men was 45 inches. Because this interval appears well in the normal stadium and because it coincides with two paces in the

8 steps per yard line system of marching, it is one of the most popular horizontal spacings used by our nation's bands.   It might also be noted that the four men needed to fill the distance from one yard-line to another at this interval equals a half rank unit for bands marching eight men abreast.   It is needless to say that this is a very desirable situation in any system of precision marching.

Vertical intervals appear well when they are at least one half again as long as its horizontal counterpart.   A horizontal interval of two paces, for instance, might well be coupled with a vertical interval of three paces.   It would be ideal to find a vertical interval which would correspond to a definite number of standard paces, while it also corresponds to the horizontal field markings (sidelines, and third stripes).   The gridiron is unfortunately not marked in a manner conducive to fulfilling this ideal.   The gridiron is 160 feet wide or 1920 inches.   It is divided into three parts by the "third stripes" or into areas 640 inches wide.   To make maximum use of these markings, our problem is to divide the field into parts which will place equally spaced men on both sidelines and the "third stripes."

If we divide the entire width, 1920 inches, into equal parts which fulfill the above requirement, we have our choice of the following intervals.

39 equal parts	49 3/13	inches apart
36 equal parts	53 1/3	inches apart
33 equal parts	58 2/11	inches apart
30 equal parts	64	inches apart
27 equal parts	71 1/9	inches apart
24 equal parts	80	inches apart
21 equal parts	90 9/21	inches apart

Unfortunately none of these intervals coincide with the 22½ inch or the 30 inch marching paces dictated by vertical field markings.   If we use multiples of the 22½ inch pace, we need a vertical interval of 22½ inches, 45 inches, 67½ inches or 90 inches.   In the 30 inch pace system, we need intervals of 30 inches, 60 inches, or 90 inches.   None of these figures coincide exactly with the intervals dictated by the field markings.   In other words pace intervals do not coincide with horizontal field markings.

The band director is forced then to choose between field markings and the advantages of standard pace.   The problem is frequently

resolved in favor of the field markings. The latter are mathematically placed, while the pace of a bandsman marching vertically without
the benefit of yardline is strictly a matter of human judgment.

If we compare the discrepancy of pace and field marking requirements, we find the following relationships.

Field Marking Intervals	*22½" Pace System*		*30" Pace System*	
(#1) 49+ inches	45 inches	(2)		
53+ inches				
58+ inches			60 inches	(2)
(#2) 64 inches	67 inches	(3)	60 inches	(2)
71+ inches	67 inches	(3)		
80 inches				
(#3) 90+ inches	90 inches	(4)	90 inches	(3)

If pace is going to conform with the 49 inches required to divide
the field into 39 equal parts, as shown in #1 above, normal paces
of 22½" must be increased approximately two inches per pace when
marching vertically. If this is standardized as normal procedure for a
given organization, two paces taken in a vertical direction will equal
one vertical interval.

Other relationships such as that shown in #3 envolves less or
no pace interval discrepancy. In #3, four paces of 22½ inches
each will equal one vertical interval or three 30 inch paces may be
used to equal one such interval.

A number of practical systems can be devised from the above
comparisons. If a band utilizes the 22½ pace system a vertical
interval of 64 inches is practical. This system envolves a slight
lengthening of vertical pace, however. It might well be coupled with
a horizontal interval of 45 inches. This, in simple terms would
represent a horizontal interval of 2 paces and a vertical one of three.
Larger bands find this combination a practical one. Jack Lee, in his
very fine book, *Modern Marching Band Techniques*, suggests the 64
inch vertical interval.

Smaller bands, however, having to make maximum use of available personnel might choose the relationships suggested in number 3. A
band marching with the 22½ inch pace might well adopt a horizon-

tal interval of 45 inches or 67½ to be coupled with a vertical interval of 90 inches. (#3)   The same group marching at a 39 inch pace might well couple a 30 inch horizontal interval with a verticle interval of 60 inches (58) or (90) inches.   In both cases the error is completely negligible.   Human error accounts for a larger discrepancy.

The system utilized by a specific band must be designed for that group.   Time spent in this selection will pay dividends in formation effectiveness.

There are several commercial charts available on the market which will serve the needs of many bands.   The choice of one of them or *none* of them must be carefully made.   It would seem better to mimeograph charts "tailor-made" for a group, rather than compromise the effectiveness of formations for the convenience of commercially prepared charts.

Once a chart and system is chosen, it must be kept constant. Each bandsman must develop the ability to align himself at a standard interval to the rear, and to the side of another bandsman.   Charting which constantly changes horizontal and vertical intervals leads only to confusion on the part of bandsman and director alike.

Common practice has ruled that any line at an angle of more than 45 degrees from the sideline be treated as a vertical line.   Those under 45 degrees are aligned with the horizontal spacing.   In actual practice, it is best for the director to consider each formation separately however.   Audience location in respect to the formation may influence his decision.   An abrupt change from one interval to another often creates the impression of a mistake for those people seated at an angle to the formation, (10 or 20 yd. lines) or those in the end zones.

Example of charts dividing the football gridiron into 24 and 30 equal parts are shown on the following page.

If the designers of marching band formations would be completely moved by the demands of perspective, intervals would constantly increase in size in proportion to their distance from the viewer. Yardlines, which are themselves subject to the taint of perspective would not be used.   Instead all vertical lines would slant away from the fortunate viewer seated on the 50 yard line.   The art of producing recognizable designs and formations on the gridiron must of necessity, however, deal with "suggestion" rather than envolved detail.   Formations composed of simple lines spaced at wide inter-

In 24 Equal Parts

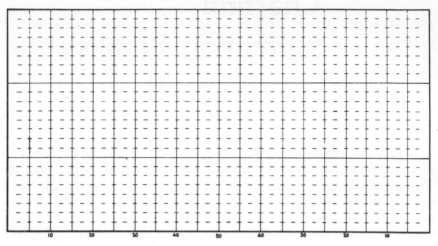

In 30 Equal Parts

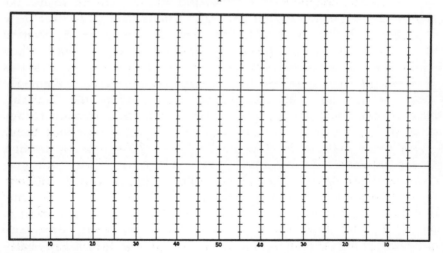

vals are more effective than those attempting to show too much detail. A well prepared charting system, assuring adequate vertical
spacing, will not solve all the problems of perspective or of legibility,
but it will serve as one of the most simple and effective means to
this end.

chapter XVI

Charting
Formation Breaks

Chapter IV defined motion between two formations as "formation breaks." Most of the material covered in this book may be adapted and applied to them. This is frequently the least developed part of the marching band halftime performance.

The traditional method of charting movement has dealt almost exclusively with the shortest route between two stationary positions in which each bandsman goes directly from an old position to a new one. This system has frequently referred to as the "splash" or "explosion" technique. To the spectator the process seems like a short period of confusion, gradually taking the form of a new formation. Action of this type between formations can be referred to as "marching" only in the most free definition of the word which might define it as a "syncronized movement of the feet." There is no distinguishable pattern, order or grouping which we commonly think of as being present in "marching." While the "splash" method is the most simple way to move from one formation to another, it does not make use of the full potential of the marching band.

Movement between formations is capable of being as interesting to the audience as is the final formation itself. When both precision motions and formations are equally emphasized a halftime performance becomes an ever evolving spectacle of design and motion. It seems unfortunate that the traditional half-time performance has not exploited this vast area. Too many times coordinated group movement is absolutely non-existant in the half-time show.

A semblance of order, balance and evolving design can easily be given to movement between formations by making the smallest unit a half rank of three or four men, rather than individual marchers.

Three men are sufficient to give the semblance of a rank. If each rank is moved as a unit, the effect is one of precision marching.

A minimum of thought reveals methods of adding balance to the motion. Ranks on opposite sides of the field, for instance, might move in or out simultaneously. A group of three men moving upfield might become a part of two or more ranks moving in the same direction. In many cases the band might move in company fronts, suddenly breaking off, through small unit turns, into position. If the case arises where a rank is already in position for the ensuing formation, it might be asked to execute a center wheel, which will add to the movement, but not take it out of position.

The problem of charting the "unit system" of formation breaks is one of charting *motion*, not merely *direction*.

Because units are being charted instead of individuals, fewer lines are necessary, but interpreting the lines may be slightly more complex. Ranks will usually move horizontally or vertically in relation to the sidelines, seldom diagonally. Motion is basically that of straight lines and unit turns of any variety.

The entire motion between two formations can usually be shown on one chart. Two charts are necessary only when the action is very complex. The figure on page 103 shows the entire action of the band moving from one formation to another. It necessarily fails to illustrate the effect of the maneuver as viewed by the spectator.

This chart was devised by superimposing the second formation on top of the first. In this case, onion skin paper, lightly marked with an identical football gridiron and bearing the second formation was placed over the first drawing. The first formation, easily visible through the paper was then transferred to the second. After careful study to determine a balanced motion the final arrows were drawn in showing the actual movement of ranks. Colors were actually used to make each design more distinct.

The author has found the use of onion skin paper of great value. It makes the process of transferring a drawing very simple. It also has the advantage of being cheap to use. As a result it makes experimentation much more practical than on expensive charts.

Charting Drills and Maneuvers

When motion becomes complex and is executed in a compact area, it is necessary to use the "series method" of charting. The latter

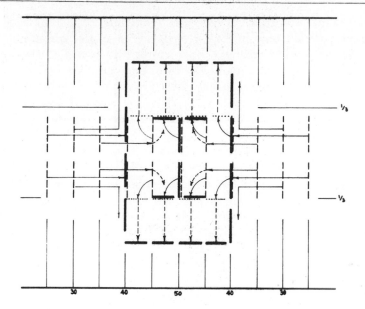

method has been used throughout this book. Chapter IX for instance, presents most of its multiple turn entrances in a series of drawings to more clearly illustrate the motion.

As in formation to formation charting, superimposition is used to illustrate and to work out each step of the motion. The old position may be shown in colors, or as a solid line moving to dotted lines or vice versa. This process is continued until the drill is completed or until the method becomes obvious.

The Section Leader System

The University of Wisconsin Marching Band during the author's tenure as its director and more recently the Drake University Marching Band has operated without the use of charts in the hands of individual bandsmen. Instead, section leaders were placed in charge of various ranks of the band. In this case "section" refers not to instruments, but to a given number of men or ranks. The section leaders assumed the responsibility for moving each unit assigned to him. Normally this was a section of three or four ranks. The section leader system was devised to more clearly show each unit not only where to go, but how to go there.

When competent students are chosen for this duty and when they thoroughly understand their assignments, formation breaks are accomplished in a minimum of time. This system has represented the quickest way to move from formation to formation. Each assignment of a section leader can usually be executed in a matter of seconds. Since all section leaders work simultaneously the total time needed to change a formation is often less than a minute.

The author does not suggest the use of this system unless competent personal is available. The section leaders must meet with the director prior to each rehearsal and thoroughly understand each performance. When this is accomplished, the rehearsal will move smoothly and efficiently.

These are some of the advantages noted using the section leader system.

1. It eliminates the problems of mis-read, lost or revised charts.
2. It is very flexible in case error does occur. Section leaders adjust readily, charts do not.
3. It provides trained leadership on the practice field to facilitate the smooth flow of a rehearsal.
4. It provides a "council" of bandsmen to work with the director in planning performances.

The Whirling Formation Technique

Few designs or maneuvers executed by the University of Wisconsin Band have caused more interest than the "whirling" formation often included in its performances. One of the first performances of this technique was included in the Rose Bowl performance of the Wisconsin Band in 1953. Its effect might be described as follows.

The band maneuvers into what appears as straight horizontal lines of various lengths and placement. Suddenly the entire pattern changes to vertical lines and back to vertical ones. Multiple ranks or segments of the band may be seen whirling around and around. The entire action suddenly reverses direction and abruptly halts. The audience startled by the abrupt halt, does a "double take" and finds the band has actually halted in a huge U. S. A. formation. Nowhere in the maneuvers, however, has the basic whirling movement ceased until the abrupt halt.

The execution of a "whirling" maneuver is not difficult.   Its secret lies in a well chosen *underlying formation*.

In preparing the maneuvers, planning must be reversed.   When the final formation has been laid out another formation, eight counts of turning motion away, is laid out.   This formation must be completely different so that it gives no indication of the final design.   It is to this underlying formation that the band maneuvers, not the final one.   The band is next thought of in terms of the segments which will eventually turn into the final design.   These segments are given a routine of turns to execute before abruptly moving into the final formation.   The motion of the turning segments is balanced or contrasted to give the most intriguing effect to the audience.   At a strategic moment in the music, the band moves neatly into the final design.

The following illustration pictures both the underlying formation and the final turn.

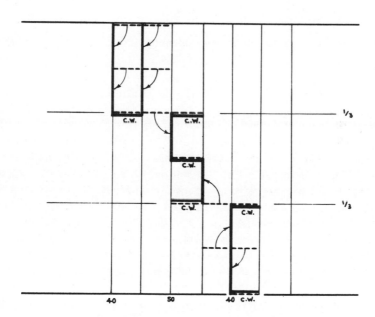

chapter XVII

Basic Drill

Basic drill, as experienced by the army rookie or the new bandsman, is the introduction to basic positions, facings, and fundamentals of marching. Basic drill for the bandsman is not confined to a "boot camp" at the beginning of his marching career. For him it is a vital part of each new season's work. A new season for the modern marching band might bring new basic movements to be learned. Many of the old fundamentals may have been changed for the sake of increased efficiency or perhaps, merely for a "new look."

In a sense the modern marching band recognizes no "correct" way of executing a fundamental. For years the Basic Manual of Close Order Drill of the U.S. Army served as the standard of "correctness," but as it has been studied critically and better ways have been found to execute specific movements, the manual has been discarded. The new fundamentals of the marching band are accepted only after they meet a standard of the practical, the efficient, and the novel. A high premium is placed on originality and variety. The best manual is "tailor-made" to the needs, capabilities, and the tastes of the individual organization.

The result of this concept, in part, has accounted for the different styles of marching bands. A great deal of emphasis has been placed by some groups on being different or something apart from the ordinary. Fortunately, bands that feel themselves in the latter category generally are blessed with a great deal of esprit de corps in their organization.

A good manual is primarily a functional one. It includes only movements which will be used frequently throughout the coming season and only those movements which are too basic to be taught as a part of a performance during the ensuing weeks. An important and fortunate part of the changing manual is the fact that it adds interest and a challenge to the returning bandsman. Basic drill is not a repeat performance for him. Progress is always in evidence. Enthusiasm is more likely to be the underlying mood rather than apathy.

The basic drill period is normally the best time to cope with individual problems. It is unfortunate that rehearsal schedules do not allow for more individual help during the season proper, but this situation can be greatly alleviated by careful attention to individual problems during the initial period of training. With this emphasis basic drill might best be handled in small groups.

Certification Drill

Certification drill is the term applied by the author to the basic drill sessions of organizations with which he has worked. Before the first full band rehearsal in the fall every member of the band has been certified as a member. It is not strange then, to see the band well trained at its very first rehearsal. Often preparation for the first performance of the season begins immediately. It is often difficult to identify the freshman from the veteran bandsman for in reality they have twice as much rehearsal time in at the time of the first rehearsal of the full band.

Basic drill is in this case composed of certification drill for the new bandsman, and refresher drill for the returning bandsman. They are conducted whenever convenient during registration week. The only real qualification of the system is that the basic drill precedes the first full rehearsal of the marching band.

The advantages of a well trained band from the first rehearsal are multiple. Initial enthusiasm is not dulled by needless drill and explanation. Each bandsman is challenged from the beginning of the rehearsal. The effect of immediate progress instead of initial sluggishness instills added enthusiasm for the work to come.

Refresher drill is normally conducted for only half of the number of hours spent in certification drill. As a rule returning bandsmen can master the new material in approximately half of the time needed by the freshman who is not familiar with the "system." These periods may be extended for the individual, however, if such seems to be necessary. All sessions are conducted by section leaders or drill instructors carefully chosen and drilled by the director. This technique has been used successfully on the high school and college level. The success, of course, is directly dependent on the selection and guidance of the student leaders. If the section leader system is to be used throughout the season, certification drill offers an excellent opportunity for the director to observe and to guide these people.

The Basic Manual

The basic manual, it has been stated, includes only the basic movements which will be used throughout the marching season. The remainder of this chapter is devoted to a listing of typical movements which might be included in a "tailor-made" manual. Several methods may be listed for any movement. It should not be understood, however, that this is a normal situation. The listing below is not a manual in itself. It is merely a list from which a manual could be devised. Once again, it is hoped that these variations will serve as food for thought from which original ideas will be suggested to the reader.

Positions

The minimum number of basic positions needed during the course of a season is probably three. The following are usually included in basic manuals.

1. Attention—The traditional position of attention is hard to improve upon. It is well, however, to hold the instruments uniformly in one hand or the other. It is not felt that a further description of this position is needed here.
2. Parade rest—Once again the traditional position is adequate. It serves as a secondary position of attention which serves to embellish the original. Both of these positions may be given more movement in their execution through knee lifts, but this phase is left to the reader's tastes.
3. At ease—The command "at ease!" or more simply, "relax" serves as a practical means for giving instruction. The position, as defined here, retains the same stance as the position from which it is given. The body muscles may be more relaxed however, and the head and eyes may turn to listen to instructions.
4. At rest—The standard position of *at-rest* might be retained as the most relaxed position of marching order.

It is normally used when long periods of waiting or in-
activity are anticipated.

Facings

While facings are important movements in the vocabulary of the
marching band, they are often used only occasionally on the football field. Three methods are given here for executing the right
face. The left face is, obviously, executed using opposite directions.

1. Right face, traditional—The traditional right face is adequate, but it is not a particularly interesting movement to see executed. A close look at the turning motion
   reveals a rather awkward appearance.
2. Right face, flank type—The basic flank pivot lends itself
   readily to facing movements. On count one, step forward with the left foot, shifting the weight of the body
   forward to the left foot. On count two, pivot 90 degrees to the right on the heel of the right foot and the
   toe of the left. On count three, bring the left foot into
   the right to a position of attention. The right foot does
   not leave the ground; it merely pivots.
3. Right face, kick style—On count one, kick the left foot
   forward while turning 90 degrees to the right. The pivot
   is on the toe of the right foot. On count two, bring the
   left foot into the right to a position of attention.

About Face

The about face is probably the most useful and the most interesting facing to view. Even though it serves no purpose, in some cases
it has been used in a sequence of two, for the sole purpose of adding
color to a segment of the performance. In actual practice the about
face movement normally finds more functional value on the football
field than the 90 degree facings.

1. About face, traditional—The traditional about face leaves
   much to be desired from the audience standpoint. It is
   awkward to execute and, for the most part, it is a smooth
   motion that does not lend itself to snap and precision.
   It may be improved somewhat by adding a step and a
   kick halt to it after the basic movement is completed.
2. About face, to-the-rear style—On count one, step forward with the left foot, shifting the weight of the body
   forward to the left foot. The left foot touches the ground
   in its extended position on count one. As it touches the
   body turns to the right 180 degrees, pivoting on the toe

of the left foot. The right foot is raised slightly in turning. It touches the ground once again on count two, this time in the new direction. On count three, the left foot is brought forward to a position of attention.

3. About face, hop style—On count one, jump straight up lifting the left foot followed by the right in such a manner that the left foot precedes and touches the ground before the right. On counts two, three, and four, execute the to-the-rear about face described above. As simple as it seems, this about face movement has been a favorite of mid-west audiences wherever it has been performed. It has served as the standard about face of the Drake Band.

4. About face, kick style—On count one, kick the right foot forward to an angle of 45 degrees from the hip. On count two, bring the foreleg back across the left leg so that it touches it lightly. The knee bends, but does not change its position on count two. On count three, turn the entire body 180 degrees to the left on the toe of the left foot. Coordinate this movement with a kick of the right leg from its second position to a position where the entire leg extends at a 45 degree angle to the right of the body after it has completed its turn. On count four, return the leg to a position of attention.

Marking Time

Marking time is a definite part of the basic manual. Like positions, and facings, it too has many variations from which a standard method might be chosen. Four variations are listed here.

1. Mark time, traditional—The traditional method of marking time requires that the toes be pointed down as the leg is raised approximately six inches. This method is very adequate. As a matter of fact, it is difficult to vary it a great deal.

2. Mark time, raised right foot—One simple way used by some groups to vary the basic method is to raise the right foot up to the horizontal while keeping the left foot constantly in a lower path. The effect when executed by a large group is quite intriguing.

3. Mark time, count sequence—A variation of the above is used by one group. On every third beat of a four count series the right leg is raised above the normal height.

4. Mark time, count sequence—On every third count of a four count series the right foot may be kicked out to the side. On count four it resumes its normal path. Groups

which have standardized this type of marking time system
insist that it is not difficult to teach.   Its effect is worth
the effort spent.

Arm Swing

In the modern marching band, arm swing is of basic importance.
It should certainly be isolated and given primary attention in the
basic manual.   It is highly desirable that all instruments be held
in the same hand allowing for maximum effect of the arm swing.

1. Arm swing, traditional—Unfortunately the traditional
   view of arm swing has been to virtually ignore it.   As the
   modern band has developed, however, it has received an
   increasing amount of attention.   The most common technique now used seems to be a forward swing of the entire
   arm to a point approximately forty-five degrees from
   the shoulder and back to a position about six inches in
   back of the body.
2. Arm swing, British style—The British style arm swing
   is the reverse of the traditional style of our country, in
   that the swing is emphasized beyond normal requirements.
   The arm is swung vigorously forward to a point prac-
   tically horizontal with the ground.   The forearm then
   bends somewhat so that arm crosses the chest slightly.
   This style has been used more and more frequently in
   our organizations.
3. Arm swing, high step style—Fast tempi have made the
   full arm swing impractical for many bands.   Groups
   using a fast tempo frequently adopt a more restricted
   swing of the arm which is held in a bent postion from the
   elbow.   The arc in this case, is as little as twenty four
   inches wide.   When the restricted swing is used the arm
   very often is not allowed to pass back behind the body.

Carriage

Body carriage is a great concern of the basic manual.   Nothing is
of more importance to the appearance of the band than the appearance of the individuals of which it is composed.   A good basic manual
must stipulate knee lift, shoulder and instrument swing, back arch
(or the lack thereof) and every detail of body position that is of
importance in presenting a good impression.   No attempt is made
here, to discuss the innumerable possibilities that have been used or
which might be created.

The first and last steps are of such importance that they might well be given treatment as a special item in the basic manual. Every drillmaster is familiar with the special problems the two steps entail. The natural tendency of the marcher is to "pussyfoot" in each case. The first and last step must be equal to the normal pace of a group, but a great deal of practice is needed to achieve this.

First and Last Steps

The first step can be a thing of beauty if it is overemphasized and executed with precision. Few first paces can equal the beauty of the "kick forward march." It is executed by kicking the left foot vigorously forward about six inches from the ground, without bending the knee, immediately on the command "march!" The foot is then lowered slowly so that it touches the ground on count one. The regular pace follows. The effect is one of extreme precision and snap when well executed.

Step-Offs

Precision marching often demands that the bandsman step off in various directions from a stationary position, without loss of pace due to special pivot procedures designed to reverse direction more smoothly. This necessitates the need for cross-over steps or kick pivots. If, for instance, a drill required the bandsman to step off to the right without loss of pace, he merely shifts his weight to the right as he crosses the left foot in front of the right taking a full pace in that direction.

A small amount of thought given to the problem of stepping off in each direction will reveal a method of accomplishing each of these movements. If it is anticipated that they will be used frequently during a season, they might well be included as a part of the basic manual.

Flank Pivots

The traditional flank pivot is difficult to improve upon, however, precision marching demands new functional pivots not listed in the traditional annals of marching.

1. Cross-over pivots—The following diagram illustrates a situation that calls of a cross-over pivot, or one other than

the traditional one. In this case the band cannot pivot
simultaneously in two directions using the standard pivot.

The cross-over pivot must be used by one half of the
band to coordinate with the standard pivot of the other
half. If the cross-over pivot is to be used for a left flank,
it is executed by bringing the right foot around the left
which pivots the weight of the body to the left as the
right foot passes. The pivot may seem awkward at first,
but it has been used by many groups with excellent results.

2. The Whirl pivot—The whirl pivot is used to accomplish
the same purpose as the cross-over pivot. A whirl pivot
to the left is accomplished when the left foot is forward.
The body pivots on the left toe and whirls 270 degrees
to the right so that at the end of the turn the right foot
is placed down one full pace in the new direction to the
left. Because the whirl pivot is an audience pleaser it
has been standardized by one group as its normal pivot.

To-the-rear Movements

The traditional to-the-rear continues to be the accepted method of
executing this movement. Many groups have standardized a turn
to the left instead of the right, however, so that the steps out in a
given direction may equal the steps back. This is not the case if
the turn is executed to the right in the traditional manner.

Two rather interesting variations of the traditional method are
listed below.

1. The anticipated turn—A few women's drill teams have
created a to-the-rear based on the traditional method, but
one which incorporates an earlier turn of the body. Normally the turn is executed to the right as the left foot
touches the ground, or is "planted." The new method
anticipates the turn so that the body is already facing
the new direction when the left foot reaches its position.
The actual turn is executed on the previous count.
The effect is one of smoothness, admirably suited to
women.

2. The Slow turn to-the-rear—The slow turn is a beautiful maneuver to see executed. It is accomplished in the traditional manner, with the exception that the body does not turn immediately at the point where the left foot is planted. Instead the bandsman marches backward taking a full step with the right and the left foot. On the third step backward, when the right foot is back, the body turns slowly to the right, completing the turn as the left foot touches the ground. The slow turn is novel and refreshing to both the audience and the marcher.

Special "Licks"

In addition to the basic requirements of marching, a few special movements, or "licks" might be used frequently enough during a season to justify their inclusion in the basic manual. A few of these are described below.

1 Fake pivots—An audience may be taken by surprise when a group fakes a pivot in one direction and actually goes in the opposite one. Surprise, it will be remembered, is one of the most effective appeals a group might make. A fake left flank is executed by pivoting to the right when the left foot is planted. On the next count, however, a to-the-rear is immediately executed reversing the direction.

2. Freezes—Freezes are very effective when used at points of a drill where they are least expected. Freezes are nothing more than an abrupt halting of the action when one foot is forward and the other back. They are particularly effective when used during silent drills, described in a previous chapter.

3. The bow—The bow is very effective when it is executed by the entire band simultaneously. It is frequently used in a series of counts, such as: bow, 2, 3, 4, up, 2, 3, 4.

4. Cap salute—Serving about the same purpose as the bow, the cap might be taken off and held in the air at a 45 degree angle to the body. Once again, this movement is best executed to a series of verbal counts.

5. Dance routines—Dance steps which might be used frequently during a season might qualify for a spot in the basic manual. There is little need that they be described here.

6. The goose step—Special steps, such as the familiar goose step, can add a great deal of interest to a performance. With the Second World War fast becoming a memory it is once again finding its way into the American repetoire of marching steps.

7. The off-beat goose step—The goose step, executed so that the foot is up on the accented beat and lowered on the second beat, is a favorite marching step of one organization. Novelty can be added to many such steps by merely reversing the traditional beat.

8. The whirl step—The whirl step is a more difficult movement to master, yet it has been executed by both large and small marching groups with excellent success. It consists of a 360 degree turn to the right between two marching steps. When the left foot is forward the body is thrown forward, in a whirling turn to the right. The pivot is obviously on the toe of the left foot. The turn must be completed when the right foot touches the ground one pace later. No steps are lost in execution.

Miscellaneous Movements

The basic manual also includes drum-major signals; bring-ups, or methods of bringing the instruments to a playing position; drum halts, roll-offs, and any other obvious fundamentals not described in the above discussion.

Outstanding
College Bands

University of Michigan Marching Band, William D. Revelli, Director

Ohio State University Marching Band, Jack Evans, Director

University of Wisconsin Marching Band at the Rose Bowl, Don R. Marcouiller, Director

State University of Iowa Marching Band, Fred Ebbs, Director

University of Minnesota Marching Band, Gale L. Sperry, Director

Michigan State University Marching Band, Leonard Falcone, Director

University of Illinois Marching Band, Everett D. Kisinger, Director

Purdue University Marching Band, Al G. Wright, Director

Northwestern University Marching Band. John Paynter, Director

Indiana "Marching Hundred," Ronald Gregory, Director

Bayless, A. J., "Showtime Stigma vs. Precision Marching"
Instrumentalist vol. 20 no. 1 (Nov. Dec. 1952) p. 12

Bennett, George T.
"Field Routines for Marching Band Contests"
Marching and Maneuvering Series, Vol. III
Chicago: Gamble Hinged Co. 1938

"Grooming the Marching Band for High School Contests"
Marching and Maneuvering Series Vol. VI 1937
Chicago: Gamble Hinged Co.

"Required and Special Maneuvers for High School March-
ing Band Contests"
Marching and Maneuvering Series, Vol. IV
Chicago: Gamble Hinged Co. 1937

Bergan, Hal
Band Pageantry
New York: Remick 1948

"Marching Band Materials"
Instrumentalist Vol. 9 no. 2 (Oct. 1954)

"On Marching Bands"
Music Journal, Jan. Feb. 1949 p. 23

Crawford, John A. and Ruddick, J. Leon
"A Pageant of Marching Bands"
Music Educators Journal Vol. XXIV Mar. 1938 p. 41

Dale, Carroll R. *Fundamentals of Drill for Marching Bands*
Chicago: Gamble Hinged Co. 1945

Dvorak, R. F. *The Band on Parade*
    Chicago: Carl Fischer Co. 1937

Ferguson, Henry "Drill and Formation Routines for the Foot-
    ball Band"
    Etude Vol. 65 Oct. 1947 p. 499

Gregory, R. D. "Let's Face the Facts About Marching Bands"
    School Musician. May 1950

Haywood, J. C. "Every Camp Needs a Drum and Bugle
    Corps"
    Music Dealer 3:13 May 1949

Hoffman, M. "I Like Bands, but"
    Music Education Magazine 30:41-4 Nov. 1950

Jones, J. P.
    "As I See the Place of Band in Marching Maneuvers"
    School Musician Jan. 1950

    "These Are Fundamentals of a First Class Marching Band"
    School Musician Sept. 1950

Jones, Stefan, *Dance Drills for Band Shows*
    Chicago: Hanson 1953

King, J. R. *Here Comes the Stunt Band*
    Berkeley, Calif. Don Keller Music Co. 1953

Lee, Jack *Modern Marching Band Techniques*
    Winona, Minn. Hal Leonard Music, Inc. 1955

Ludwig, W. F. "Let's Organize a Drum Corps"
    Elkhart: W. F. Ludwig Drum Co. 1951

Oldfield, Willis P. *Twenty and Seven Drill Band Maneuvers*
    New York: Mills Music Corp. 1944

Righter, Charles B. *Gridiron Pageantry*
    Chicago: Carl Fischer, Inc. 1946

Righter, Charles B. "How To Kill the Marching Band"
    Instrumentalist Vol. IV May 1950

Smith, Claude   *Practical Stunts and Evolutions for the Band and Drum and Bugle Corps*
Chicago: Gamble Hinged Co.   1935

Wettlaufer, J. Maynard
Building a Show Band
Chicago: Belwin, Inc.   1948

"Improve the Show Band"
School Coach   Sept. 1950

Woodward, W. H.   "Drum and Bugle Corps"
School Musician   Nov. 1951

Woods, Stanley   "Bugles, Ancient and Modern"
Etude   Dec. 1951